The Greatest Mysteries of the Ancient World: Stonehenge, the Sphinx, and the Hanging Gardens of Babylon

By Charles River Editors

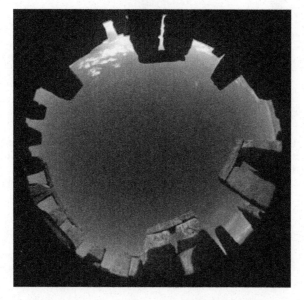

Looking up to the sky from the middle of Stonehenge

About Charles River Editors

Charles River Editors provides superior editing and original writing services across the digital publishing industry, with the expertise to create digital content for publishers across a vast range of subject matter. In addition to providing original digital content for third party publishers, we also republish civilization's greatest literary works, bringing them to new generations of readers via ebooks.

Sign up here to receive updates about free books as we publish them, and visit Our Kindle Author Page to browse today's free promotions and our most recently published Kindle titles.

Introduction

Stonehenge during the Summer Solstice in 2005

Stonehenge

"The interest that has always attached itself to Stonehenge has, without doubt, been in a great measure due to the mystery as to the origin of this unique monument of bygone time." – H.P. Blackmore, 1916.

On the Salisbury Plain, only a few hours from the hustle and bustle of Central London, remains one of the greatest surviving relics of humanity's ancient past: the mighty stone circle of Stonehenge. Stonehenge is one of the most well-known ancient sites in the world, and an image of it raises numerous associations and emotional responses. Its impressiveness comes not only from its size and remarkable level of preservation, but more so because of the incredible precision with which it was constructed during an era of simple technology and social organization. Obviously, it is a place of great importance—then and now.

Despite its placid, changeless appearance, Stonehenge has been a place of political, ideological and religious struggle for centuries. From the vigorous debates of 19th century theorists to the all-night dance parties of the 1980s, the history and legacy of Stonehenge is as much about the desires and fears of the people of modern Britain as it is about the ancients. Stonehenge has belonged to all of Britain's people since its construction began roughly 5,000 years ago, and they have all added to its unfolding story.

Of course, Stonehenge has long fascinated the rest of the world too, as people continue to try to understand every aspect of the site and the underlying purpose of it. This involves an understanding of why Stonehenge is located where it is, what the materials consist of, and what archaeology has uncovered about the people who built it. On top of that, Stonehenge is a center of mythology and folklore that has evolved over time, establishing the foundation for a unique spiritual belief system that both celebrates Stonehenge as a "living temple" and challenges the official guardians of the place.

This book comprehensively covers the facts, mysteries, and theories surrounding the ancient megalith. Readers will understand Stonehenge from all dimensions: as a physical place, an object of scholarly study, a site of ecstatic worship, a "must see" world-class tourist destination and a simultaneous icon of both history and counterculture. Along with pictures and a bibliography, you will learn about Stonehenge like you never have before.

The Sphinx

The Sphinx, with the pyramid of Khafre in the background

"It is the antiquity of the Sphinx which thrills us as we look upon it, for in itself it has no charms. The desert's waves have risen to its breast, as if to wrap the monster in a winding-sheet of gold. The face and head have been mutilated by Moslem fanatics. The mouth, the beauty of whose lips was once admired, is now expressionless. Yet grand in its loneliness, – veiled in the mystery of unnamed ages, – the relic of Egyptian antiquity stands solemn and silent in the presence of the awful desert – symbol of eternity. Here it disputes with Time the empire of the past; forever gazing on and on into a future which will still be distant when we, like all who have preceded us and looked upon its face, have lived our little lives and disappeared." – John Lawson Stoddard, 1898

One of the oldest and most famous statues of the world, the Great Sphinx at Giza has fascinated people for thousands of years. While the sphinx was a well known mythological creature among various ancient civilizations, the Egyptian statue that is now most famously associated with the creature is full of mysteries that have been endlessly debated throughout the centuries and continue to be hotly contested among scholars.

The famous "Riddle of the Sphinx", told by Sophocles in his play Oedipus Rex in the 5th century B.C., characterized the sphinx as a clever and powerful creature, and even today young kids learn about the story. But the mysteries of the Egyptian statue were discussed even among the ancient Romans; Pliny the Elder, the famous Roman author and philosopher killed in Pompeii during the eruption of Mount Vesuvius in 79 A.D., wrote in his *Natural Histories* that contemporary Egyptians considered the Sphinx a "divinity" and "that King Harmais was buried in it".

Nearly 2,000 years later, people still wonder about the origins of the statue, but most believe it was constructed around the middle of the 3rd millennium B.C. As anyone who has seen the statue is now aware, it has suffered weatherization damage, and even the sources of the damage has been debated and turned into the stuff of legend, as evidenced by the story of Napoleon's French soldiers shooting off the Sphinx's nose. In conjunction with that, there are mysteries over the archaeological history of the statue, including whether the ancient Egyptians themselves attempted to excavate the Sphinx and clear the sands that were beginning to cover it up.

The Great Sphinx at Giza continues to be a source of endless fascination and mystery, but everyone can agree that it is a marvelous and interesting structure. *History's Greatest Mysteries:* This book comprehensively covers the facts, mysteries, and theories surrounding the ancient statue and the mythological creature the statue was modeled after. Along with pictures and a bibliography, you will learn about the Sphinx like you never have before, in no time at all.

The Hanging Gardens of Babylon

A 16th-century colored engraving of the Hanging Gardens of Babylon by Dutch artist Martin Heemskerck, with the Tower of Babel in the background

"There was also, beside the acropolis, the Hanging Garden, as it is called, which was built, not by Semiramis, but by a later Syrian king to please one of his concubines; for she, they say, being a Persian by race and longing for the meadows of her mountains, asked the king to imitate, through the artifice of a planted garden, the distinctive landscape of Persia." Diodorus Siculus

In antiquity, the Hanging Gardens, like the Great Pyramid of Giza, were considered both a technological marvel and an aesthetic masterpiece. Ancient historians believed that the Hanging Gardens were constructed around the 7th century B.C. after the second rise of Babylon, which would make them the second-oldest of the Seven Wonders of the Ancient World. Reputedly, they were created by the biblical Nebuchadnezzar II (the king who conquered Judea) to please his homesick wife, after the model of Egyptian pleasure gardens, but in 1993, British Assyriologist, Stephanie Dalley, proposed a theory that they were ordered built by the Assyrian King Sennacherib a century earlier for his giant palace at Nineveh, instead. She believed that the two sites were easily confused by ancient sources, resulting in the Gardens being incorrectly located in Babylon a century later.

Many ancient writers discussed the Hanging Gardens, including Strabo, Diodorus Siculus, and Quintus Curtius Rufus. In fact, Diodorus Siculus and Philo of Byzantium both described the mechanisms of the Gardens at length. According to their accounts, the Hanging Gardens were terraced and cultivated orchards that were built over a series of buildings made of glazed ceramic and perhaps watered by some kind of pulley or pump system of irrigation. Water was drawn from a reservoir through a network of reeds and bricks, held together by asphalt and cement, with lead used as a sealant. The Gardens were built on a citadel 80 feet high with walls 22 feet thick.

Despite the detailed descriptions, historians still question whether the Hanging Gardens ever actually existed. The sheer amount of water that would've been required, and the fact that they would've relied on technology that was supposedly invented 400 years down the line cast doubt upon their existence. Officially, the reason why it is not known whether the Hanging Gardens ever existed is because they were reported to have been destroyed by several earthquakes, the last of which left the Hanging Gardens completely ruined by the 2nd century B.C., around the time the Greek "tourists" were writing their pamphlets. Therefore, it is not known if any of the writers who described them ever truly saw the Hanging Gardens, and even as ancient Greeks and Romans of different centuries wrote about the Hanging Gardens and relied on previous ancient texts, Babylonian sources do not mention them. Neither do near-contemporaneous Greek sources like Herodotus.

This book comprehensively covers the history and mystery of the famous wonder of the ancient world, looking at ancient descriptions of the Hanging Gardens and the questions modern academics are still trying to answer. Along with pictures and a bibliography, you will learn about the Hanging Gardens like you never have before, in no time at all.

Stonehenge

A 17th century depiction of Stonehenge

A Key to the Archaeological Terms at Stonehenge

Aubrey Holes: A series of postholes found around the outer edge of the Henge marking places where wooden poles once stood. They were named after the archaeologist John Aubrey, who is said to have discovered them.

Avenue: A pathway formed out of two embankments and accompanying standing stones that extends eastwards from Stonehenge. On the Summer Solstice, the sun rises along the Avenue. Today the Avenue is cut off from the Henge by route A344.

Axis: The alignment of Stonehenge's primary trilithons, the Avenue and the Heelstone along the line of sunrise/set on the summer and winter solstices.

Barrow: An artificial hill raised over a neolithic tomb. Found in great density around Stonehenge.

Bluestone: A non-local stone found within Stonehenge. They are smaller than the local sarsen stones.

Heelstone, The: A lone sarsen standing outside the main henge, but lying along the line of the Axis.

Henge: A circle of standing stones regardless of size.

Megalith: Any large ("mega") stones ("liths") used for the construction of monuments or buildings; especially used for ancient structures like Stonehenge.

Sarsen: A variety of hard local stones used to construct the primary ring and the trilithons of Stonehenge. The largest stones in the monument.

Trilithon: The central objects of Stonehenge, these are five sets of three sarsens: two uprights and one lintel. Arranged in a horseshoe around the Axis, they are the largest constructs at the site.

Chapter 1: Physical Description

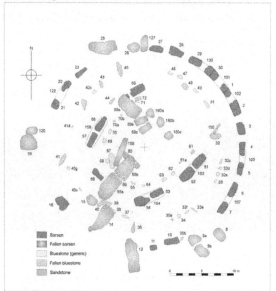

A layout of Stonehenge and its different physical characteristics, by Anthony Johnson

"Salisbury Cathedral and its neighbour Stonehenge are two eminent monuments of art and rudeness, and may show the first essay and the last perfection in architecture." – A letter written by a Dr. Johnson in 1783.

While much is disputed about the history and future of Stonehenge, there is a universal understanding of exactly what it is: the most impressive megalithic monument in Britain and possibly the world. Moreover, there is an understanding that the Stonehenge we see today is not the product of a single designer, or even a single civilization, but instead a place of importance for centuries if not millennia.

Even before construction began at the site known as Stonehenge, the locals were busy nearby. Archaeology has found the existence of construction that involved wooden posts dating back to nearly 8000 B.C. The posts had an east-west alignment similar to sites of the same nature found in Scandinavia, but not in Britain itself.

About 5,500 years ago, the Stonehenge Cursus was built a little less than half a mile to the north of Stonehenge, possibly because the woods were being cleared by farmers in that direction as the area was developed. The Cursus is a ditch that runs over a mile long and is about 150 feet wide, and the fact that it was initially thought to be an Ancient Roman race track gave it the name cursus (Latin for "course"). One of the tools presumably used to help dig the cursus was found by archaeologists, who were able to radiocarbon date it to the middle of the 4th millennium B.C.

The Stonehenge Cursus

The first Stonehenge, with construction beginning over 5,000 years ago, is believed to have been a circular earthen wall and ditch called an "embankment". The ditch and wall had a diameter of over 350 feet and two entrances in the south and northeast. Archaeology found animal bones and tools, but the fact that the tools and bones were not the same age indicated that the space was being used for burial.

The outer edge of the structure had 56 pits in a ring within the embankment, and it is now believed to have had 56 wooden posts to go along with those pits. These were called Aubrey Holes after John Aubrey, a 17th century man who specialized in antiques and first noted the existence of the pits. Some people believe that the pits held the first "blue stones", which means stone construction started at Stonehenge about 500 years earlier than commonly believed today.

Nevertheless, most people believe that the wood posts and the wood buildings constructed within the circle were removed when the first stones began being used, around 2600 B.C.

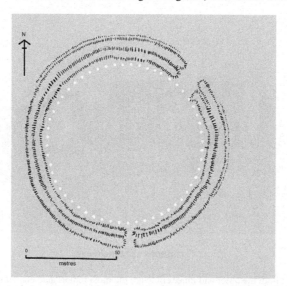

A diagram of the initial construction at Stonehenge, usually referred to as Stonehenge 1

In place of the wood buildings, the builders made two semi-circles of small "blue stones," but those were replaced only a century later with a full circle of mighty sarsen stones. These 30 upright stones each weighed about 25 tons and are believed to have come from the vicinity of the sister stone circle of Avebury, located some 20 miles away in the Marlborough Downs. They were used to construct a circle about 100 feet across. Along the top of the upright sarsens were placed "lintel" stones, which connected the ring. Despite the fact that the site was built on a slight slope, the builders managed to adjust the heights of the sarsens so that the lintels were almost level across the entire structure.

Finally, in the heart of the circle stand the mightiest of the constructions: five "trilithons" (Greek for "having three stones"). These were freestanding trios of stones with two uprights and one lintel, and the five trilithons formed a rough horseshoe. While the lintels of the sarsen circle were roughly 16 feet above the ground, the tallest trilithon was about 25 feet high. The engineering needed to construct the site is even more impressive when considering that roughly a third of the length of each upright is buried in the earth.

Trilithons at Stonehenge

The sarsens in both the outer and inner circle are the most remarkable element of the construction. They were not quarried but were instead found half-buried as boulders on the landscapes, remnants of the last Ice Age. Formed of sands bound together with silica, these stones are notably hard and are often used for roadside curbs or stone stairs. The fact that these stones were not only transported from the Marlborough Downs but also shaped into uniform rectangular forms using only stone, wood and bone tools is a testament to both the ingenuity and dedication of the builders.

Graffiti found on one of the sarsen stones

Within both the outer circle of sarsen stones and the inner horseshoe of trilithons are rings of smaller non-local stones called "blue stones." These stones vary in origin and are not as carefully worked as the sarsens. The source of many of them, however, has been traced to an area of southern Wales nearly 150 miles away. Whether they were brought by humans or glaciers to the area is still up for discussion, as archaeologists have only been able to demonstrate that either answer is within the realm of possibility. 150 miles would have required Herculean efforts to transport the stones by water and/or land, but it's apparent that some of the large stones were transported nearly two dozen miles too.

Some of Stonehenge's bluestones

The alignment of Stonehenge is of crucial importance, both for its builders and for its admirers today. The horseshoe of the trilithons looks directly towards the opening of the embankment, which itself leads to a long avenue of approach. Together, this alignment is known as the "Axis", and on this avenue is another sarsen, the famous "Heelstone." The Trilithons, Avenue and Heelstone are all aligned so that on the day of the Summer Solstice (June 21), the sun rises directly over the Heelstone, and on the Winter Solstice (December 21), it sets between the stones of the now-fallen central, tallest Trilithons. At the same time, a growing body of evidence suggests that ancient peoples only came to Stonehenge during the Winter Solstice, based in part on the discovery of pigs' teeth and an analysis of how old the pigs were when they were slaughtered.

The Heelstone

Looking at Stonehenge from the Heelstone

While there is a possibility that other stones are similarly aligned with other celestial events so that the entire building was a rough calendar of the year, these associations are still debated by archaeologists. The field of archaeoastronomy (the study of the relationship between ancient peoples and the stars) at Stonehenge has been a contentious one, with astronomers and archaeologists taking sides originally around *Stonehenge Decoded* (1963) by Gerald Hawkins, which claimed Stonehenge could be used to predict eclipses. The debates began centuries ago, with even Edmund Halley studying the placement of the Heelstone and debating whether it had been astronomically aligned or even with the help of a magnetic compass.

Stonehenge rests on the Salisbury Plain, a broad, high chalkland in southwestern Britain that is rich in ancient sites. Salisbury Plain includes not only the main complex at Stonehenge but also barrows, hills, palisades and other monuments. In the words of UNESCO, "they form landscapes without parallel" and are today largely protected within the World Heritage Site.[1]

This landscape is often overlooked by today's tourists, who focus upon the stones, but it was undoubtedly important for the builders and for archaeologists attempting to understand the social context in which Stonehenge was constructed. Currently, the owner of the surrounding area, the National Trust, is working to restore the ancient ecosystem: a "calcareous (chalk) grassland."

---

1 "Stonehenge, Avebury and Associated Sites. UNECO World Heritage Site Description" accessed online at http://whc.unesco.org/

This ecosystem is characterized by a thin soil over limestone or chalk bedrock and covered in hardy grasses. It is notable for its rich wildflowers, and this ecosystem was created in the Stonehenge area once it was first cleared of trees. The area will be used for grazing without harming the system,[2] but the fact that it has little in the way of fertility has actually served the site (and especially the surrounding minor sites) well, protecting them from the destruction of the plow and modern buildings that have eliminated archaeological sites in many other areas of Britain.

One area of recent landscape research has been the large number of burials on the surrounding uplands, which people have long associated with Stonehenge itself as a result. The earliest groups, those who perhaps erected the first embankments and wooden posts, buried their dead in great communal graves, such as West Kennet Long Barrow northwest of Stonehenge. In this barrow (an artificial hill with burial chambers build within), bones were mixed between individuals with different types of bones inhabiting different rooms.[3] Importantly, the builders were able to move large sarsens to create a doorway to the tomb similar to the later trilithons. However, the builders of the later Stonehenge buried their dead in individual round barrows on hilltops, often within sight of the henge. Many of these burials were of wealthy individuals, indicating that the area either had a concentration of wealth or that the powerful sought to be buried near the famous monument. For some archaeologists, this landscape was the "Lourdes" of ancient Europe, attracting (like the modern French sanctuary) numerous sick and wounded seeking healing, especially amongst the neolithic well-to-do. Some of these individuals were not healed, accounting for the high percentage of burials in the nearby area that contain these types of remains.[4] Perhaps most interestingly, archaeologists have found no evidence of burials among the barrows within the Stonehenge site itself

---

2 "BBC Nature: Chalk Grassland" accessed online at: http://www.bbc.co.uk/nature/habitats/Calcareous_grassland; and "Stonehenge Landscape Restoration Project" accessed online at: http://www.thenakedscientists.com/HTML/content/interviews/interview/1818/
3 "History and Research: West Kennet Long Barrow" on the website for English Heritage. Accessed online at http://www.english-heritage.org.uk/daysout/properties/west-kennet-long-barrow/history-and-research/
4 "Stonehenge was 'Lourdes of Prehistoric Europe,' Claim archaeologists" by Maev Kennedy in *The Guardian*, 22 Sept 2008. Accessed online at: http://www.guardian.co.uk/science/2008/sep/22/archaeology

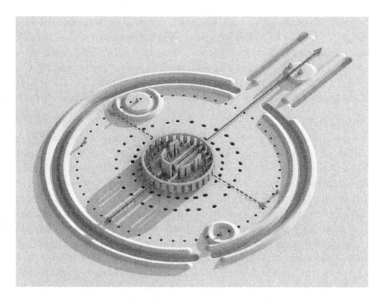

A computer rendering of what Stonehenge might have looked like when it was completed

Chapter 2: Archaeological Work

This picture during World War I shows work being done on Stonehenge, with wood propped up against some of the stones.

There has never been a point in British history where knowledge of Stonehenge was lost, so unlike other famous sites like as Lascaux Cave in France, Machu Picchu in Peru or Great

Zimbabwe, there is no revelatory moment of discovery or an accompanying transformation of archaeology. On the contrary, Stonehenge has existed in the public consciousness throughout the entire history of the discipline of archaeology, and due in part to its proximity to great universities at Oxford, Cambridge and London, Stonehenge has been intimately involved in the evolution of the discipline at every stage.

"Early" archaeology at the site can be found amongst the first attempts to apply the scientific method to the material remains of the past. The first individual who would fit this designation of "archaeologist" and who studied the site was John Aubrey. Aubrey's magnum opus was *Monumenta Britannica*, an attempt to catalog the stone monuments of southern Britain. In it, he described Stonehenge in great detail, including noting the holes where the ancient wooden posts had once been located (now called "Aubrey Holes" in his honor) and attempting to link the site up with existing textual evidence. This led him to connect the site with the Druids described by Roman chroniclers, a connection that current scholars have refuted. Nevertheless, Aubrey's work was an important step in making people look at Stonehenge as a site of scientific and historical significance, not simply one for folklore and romance.[5]

John Aubrey

After Aubrey, the next major archaeologist to work on the site was William Stukeley, who bridged the worlds of archaeology and neo-druidry. For Stukeley, an Anglican Priest, there was

---

5   *John Aubrey and Stone Circles: Britain's First Archaeologist from Avebury to Stonehenge* (2010) by Aubrey Burl. Published by Amberley Publishing, London.

no doubt the druids had built the site, and he and his contemporaries (like Iolo Morganwg in Wales) attempted to reconstruct this ancient "authentic" British religious tradition, which he believed was itself part of an ancient "universal" religion.[6] Stukeley, however, was important in the field of archaeology too, since he was the first to scientifically attempt to date the site using now-disproved theories about the migration of the magnetic poles. Despite using flawed science, Stukeley was the first to recognize the site's celestial alignment, and he even began tentative steps at excavation, opening a grave he described as belonging to a "warrior princess." Stukeley's major work on the site was entitled *Stonehenge, a Temple Restor'd to the British Druids* (1740).[7]

Stukeley

In the 19th century, excavation began in earnest not only at Stonehenge but also among the surrounding landscape, which included a large number of barrows. Two prominent figures were

---

6 *William Stukeley: Science, Religion and Archaeology in Eighteenth-Century England* (2002) by David Boyd Haycock. Boydell and Brewer Ltd.

7 A transcription of Stukeley's *Stonehenge* with modern commentary can be found at: The Internet Sacred Text Archive. Accessed online at http://www.sacred-texts.com/neu/eng/str/index.htm

William Cunnington and his patron and collaborator Sir Richard Colt Hoare. Together and separately, the two men excavated hundreds of burials and dug into the earth around the stones. While their techniques were relatively crude, and they discarded much that would be immensely useful for today's archaeologists (including ashes from campfires and both human and animal bones), a lot of what they found is still useful to researchers today. Their work *Ancient Wiltshire* (1812-21) "set a new standard in the publication of antiquities"[8] in the way that it based its findings entirely upon the concrete facts found within excavation and through its meticulous description of those findings and their contexts. These findings excited interest in the ancient past throughout Britain and served to push archaeology from the realm of antiquarian dabbling into the science that it would become.

Monument to Hoare in Salisbury Cathedral

The last of these classic archaeologists to work in the site were William Gowland and William Hawley. Gowland worked to restore the site in 1901, and Hawley attempted to do the same from 1919-1926. They stabilized stones and performed some archaeology on the site, working as agents of the state with their work being funded by public money. The site had already become a

8 "Highlights of the British Museum: The Stockbridge Urn." Accessed online at:
   http://www.britishmuseum.org/explore/highlights/highlight_objects/pe_prb/t/the_stockbridge_urn.aspx

major tourist attraction, in large part because of the Romantic images promoted by the earlier archaeologists at the site, and the state wanted to ensure their safety (from falling stones) and the maintenance of the location. Work of this nature was going on around Britain for some time, especially after Lanyon Quoit (another form of stone monument) in Cornwall tumbled in 1815. Lanyon Quoit was re-erected in 1824 by British naval engineers who took the liberty of cutting down the stones to increase their stability.[9] Similarly, Gowland re-set one of the stones using concrete and moved it roughly half a meter from its original site.

Gowland

9 "Site Focus: Lanyon Quoit" from The Heritage Journal Online. Accessed online at: http://heritageaction.wordpress.com/2010/07/25/site-focus-on-lanyon-quoit/

An 1877 picture of Stonehenge

A picture of Stonehenge from that same angle today indicates the differences created by reconstruction.

By the 1920s, archaeology was emerging into its own right, particularly the development of stratigraphy and typology. Stratigraphy is the study of soil layers at a site to determine when features were created relative to one another and to features and artifacts in other archaeological sites. Typology is the comparison of artifacts from numerous sites to determine relationships (e.g. "people from culture A produced hand axe style A and pot style C"). When used in concert, these scientific methods transformed archaeology from being the study of unique sites to allow for the understanding of the relationships between multiple sites. In Britain, the "father" of these techniques was William Flinders Petrie, who worked primarily in Egypt but began his career as a young man digging at Stonehenge in 1872 (at age 19). This technique was further revolutionized by an Australian named V. Gordon Childe who worked in the ancient ruins on the Scottish Orkney Islands. Childe aimed to transform archaeology into the study of social history of non-literate peoples.[10]

As always, Stonehenge was important in these transformations, and William Hawley was something of a transitional figure. On the one hand, he re-discovered the excavations of his predecessors by literally digging the ground they had disturbed, but he also discovered a layer he called the "Stonehenge Layer", which he dated to the construction of the sarsens. He correctly noted that many of the features (like the Aubrey Holes) pre-dated this construction, thus making him the first scholar to correctly understand that the site was constructed in several phases. In fact, a heavily modified form of his chronology is still used today. Unfortunately for Hawley, his findings were dismissed in his own time.

The multi-stage construction of Stonehenge was further developed, popularized and pushed into the realm of scientific consensus by one of the 20th century's greatest Stonehenge archaeologists: Richard Atkinson. Starting in the 1940s, Atkinson worked on excavations at the site throughout the 50s, 60s and 70s, and continued writing about it throughout his life. His last book on the subject, *Stonehenge and Neighboring Monuments*, was published in 1993, one year before his death. In 1979, Atkinson proposed an elaborate timeline for the evolution of the site (building off of Hawley's rudimentary finds), stretching from 2,800 BC to 400 AD   . Moreover, Atkinson was influential beyond Stonehenge, as he codified the techniques he used at the site in his 1953 textbook *Field Archaeology*, which was widely used in British archaeological classrooms and was republished in 1981 by Hyperion Press.

Another area that produced photogenic results during this period but unfortunately little in the way of concrete facts is experimental archaeology. This is a branch of archaeology where researchers attempt to reconstruct the tools and techniques of extinct cultures. It first came to prominence in 1947, when the Norwegian Thor Heyerdahl floated his raft "Kon-Tiki" from Peru to Easter Island to show that it was possible that the islands could have been settled by South Americans. This style of archaeology has been popular at Stonehenge because of the huge technical questions at the site: how were the stones transported, shaped, and erected?

At Stonehenge, experimental archaeologists have used elaborate pulleys to lift concrete replicas of the trilithons, attempted to drag bluestones from Wales, and even tested a theory that the stones were moved on huge stone "ball bearings."[11] While this makes for good television[12]

---

10 *A History of Archaeological Thought* (2006) by Bruce G. Trigger. Cambridge, UK: Cambridge University Press.
11 See "Stonehenge Built with Balls?" by Kate Ravilious for *National Geographic News*, December 10th, 2010. Accessed online at http://news.nationalgeographic.com/news/2010/12/101210-stonehenge-balls-ball-bearings-science-rolled/

and can sometimes disprove the feasibility of various theories, experimental archaeology in this form can never prove exactly how Stonehenge was constructed, only how it was not. Lately, experimental archaeology has moved towards trying to reconstruct the lives of the builders, not just their construction methods. The Neolithic Houses Project attempts to reconstruct the homes of the builders (based off of finds at the nearby site of Durrington Wells) and have live interpreters attempt to perform all of the basic activities of life (cooking, making tools, farming, etc) in the buildings.[13] This is part of the post-Childe move in archaeology away from the spectacular sites and into the reconstruction of ancient lives and communities.

The development of modern archaeology has been incredibly important in re-shaping recent opinion about the site. The use of chemical analysis has helped fuel the growing interest in reconstructing pre-historic landscapes. Chemical analysis' most famous technique is carbon dating, the use of Carbon 14 residues in prehistoric organic matter to determine the precise date when the once-living creature died, but it has had numerous applications across archaeology. The modern archaeologist is often as much a chemist as an excavator. Chemical dating techniques have given archaeologists a formerly-impossible Holy Grail: a precise date for historic structures and activities.

A site of such prominence as Stonehenge was ripe for chemical dating, but unfortunately, stone is not conducive to radiocarbon testing. Thus, radiocarbon dating was only applied to residue found under the stones in 1995, some 36 years after the invention of the process. Together with further investigations in 2008, archaeologists have been able to affix more precise dates to Atkinson's 1979 chronology, pushing back first construction to approximately 3000 BC.[14]

While this work, done primarily at the main Stonehenge site, has caught considerable media attention[15], other archaeologists have been working hard to expand the very concept of "Stonehenge" beyond the stones to embrace the landscape around the site, including the nearby stone circle of Avebury. While archaeologists have been interested in the surrounding areas as early as Gowland and Hawley's excavations of surrounding tombs, it has been a subject of further interest in recent years for a number of reasons.

---

12 For instance, the erection of the concrete trilithon was filmed for the American television series NOVA, in the episode "Secrets of Lost Empires – Stonehenge" (11 February 1997).

13 "Neolithic Houses Project" on the English Heritage Website. Accessed online at http://www.english-heritage.org.uk/daysout/properties/stonehenge/our-plans/our-proposals/new_external_gallery/ and the Neolithic Houses Project Blog, accessed online at http://neolithichouses.wordpress.com/

14 "Stonehenge remodelled" (2008) by Darvill et al. in the journal *Antiquity* 86:1026

15 For example, "Dig pinpoints Stonehenge origins" by James Morgan of the BBC News on September 21st 2008 (http://news.bbc.co.uk/2/hi/7625145.stm) and "New Light on Stonehenge" by Dan Jones in the North American *Smithsonian Magazine* (October 2008) (http://www.smithsonianmag.com/history-archaeology/light-on-stonehenge.html)

Stone circle at Avebury

Perhaps the most pressing issue is the deplorable state of the site. For years, the UN World Heritage Site authority, archaeologists and neo-pagan groups have protested that the nearby roads are potentially damaging the site, and one literally cuts through Stonehenge's processional avenue. Even English Heritage, the site's caretaker, now admits that changes are necessary.[16]

Aerial view of Stonehenge

This activism has led the interested parties to call for a reconstruction of the Neolithic landscape, but that only raises questions about exactly what the Neolithic landscape looked like. Modern archaeological techniques allow for more knowledge to come from the analysis of ancient pollen and wood ash, which has allowed archaeologists to describe the landscape that the builders saw: hardwood oak forests, rich in game. These approaches culminated in the final

---

16 "Why Do We Need Improvements at Stonehenge?" at English Heritage's Website. Accessed online at
   http://www.english-heritage.org.uk/daysout/properties/stonehenge/our-plans/need-for-improvement/

years of the 20th century with works like *Reconstructing Iron Age Societies: New Approaches to the British Iron Age* (1997) edited by Adam Gwilt and Colin Haselgrove, and *Stonehenge in its Landscape: Twentieth Century Excavations* (1995), edited by Rosamund M.J. Cleal, K.E. Walker and R. Montague.[17] Even more recently, the use of Global Positional Satellites (GPS) and computerized mapping technologies like Geographic Information Systems (GIS) have allowed archaeologists to plot out the locations of sites and compare various forms of data to reconstruct maps of what the builder's landscapes looked like.[18]

The growing consensus is that the site as people recognize it today was only the focal point for what served as the most important funerary landscape for its builders, like the chapel at the heart of a cemetery. For instance, the 2003-2008 Stonehenge Riverside Project found that funerary rites were central to the site from its earliest incarnation, and that it probably served as the ceremonial burial place for its society's most important and wealthiest individuals.[19] This work has also led to the discovery of vitally important sites on the nearby landscape, including the neolithic village at Durrington Walls,[20] a second neolithic stone and wood henge about half a mile from Stonehenge itself that has since been buried under the soil (and discovered using ground-penetrating radar),[21] and a third henge called "Bluestonehenge". Bluestonehenge is roughly a mile away from Stonehenge alongside the Avenue that leads from Stonehenge along the axis of the solstice,[22] while some archaeologists claim the second Neolithic henge is actually the remains of a barrow. These finds and their accompanying debates, all made within the last 10 years, suggest that the Stonehenge Landscape is only now beginning to be understood, and that a greater understanding of the site will come with further research.

---

17 *Stonehenge in its Landscape* was a crucially important work which combines all of the previous research and provides the first complete resource for the stratigraphy of the site. See Christopher Chippendale's 1995 editorial on the subject in the journal *Antiquity* #69, pages 863-865 for more information.
18 For instance, visit English Heritage's "Stonehenge WHS Interactive Map" for a relatively simple example. http://www.english-heritage.org.uk/daysout/properties/stonehenge/world-heritage-site/map/
19 "Stonehenge: one of our largest excavations draws to a close" (2008) by Mike Pitts in the journal *British Archaeology* V 102: pp 13
20 "Huge Settlement Unearthed at Stonehenge Complex" 30 Jan 2007 on ScienceDaily.com. Accessed online at: http://www.sciencedaily.com/releases/2007/01/070130191755.htm
21 "A New Henge Discovered at Stonehenge" 22 Jul 2010. University of Birmingham Website. Accessed online at: http://www.birmingham.ac.uk/schools/iaa/departments/archaeology/news/2010/new-henge.aspx
22 "Mini Stonehenge Find 'Important'" 3 Oct 2009, on BBC News. Accessed online at: http://news.bbc.co.uk/2/hi/uk_news/england/wiltshire/8288567.stm

Excavation at Durrington Walls

A computer rendering of Bluestonehenge

Chapter 3: Folklore and History

The presence of Stonehenge on the Salisbury Plain has always been public knowledge in Britain, and speculation about the site has always accompanied that site. One of the earliest written accounts is Geoffrey of Monmouth's *Historia Regum Britanniae* (cir. 1136) ("History of the Kings of Britain"), which credits the site's construction to the wizard Merlin. According to the legend, Merlin brought the stones over from Ireland either by magic or with the help of giants.[23] Theories continued to be expounded as the centuries passed, including one by the famous architect Inigo Jones, whose employees surveyed the site in 1655. Jones declared that it was most likely a Roman temple.[24] Nevertheless, until the 19th century, Stonehenge was rarely considered more than a curiosity and was not a major tourist or pilgrimage site.

This 12th century manuscript illustration depicts a giant helping Merlin build Stonehenge. It is the earliest known depiction of Stonehenge in history.

Despite these mysterious legends and wild conjectures, the site's history dating back to the Norman period is well known because it is located in an area that has been extensively farmed for centuries. It entered the history of land tenure as part of the estate of Amesbury Abbey, then transferred during the Reformation to the Earl of Hartford. Stonehenge then passed through

23 A digitalized English translation of Monmouth's work can be found at Google Books here:
http://books.google.com.co/books?id=FUoMAAAAIAAJ&printsec=frontcover&dq=geoffrey+of+monmouth&a s_brr=3&redir_esc=y#PPP7,M1 . The story of Merlin and Stonehenge can be found in Book 8, Chapter 10.
24 *A vindication of Stone-Heng restored in which the orders and rules of architecture observed by the ancient Romans are discussed: together with the customs and manners of several nations of the world in matters of building of greatest antiquity: as also, an historical narration of the most memorable of the Danes in England,* by John Webb, (1665). Printed by R. Davenport for Tho. Bassett: London.)

several other hands and into the Antrobus family, whose last heir died in World War I. It was bought in auction by a local baronet who donated it to the State.

Farm carts going past Stonehenge in the 1880s.

While Stonehenge is now officially owned by the Crown, the state has had several entities manage the site. It is currently managed by English Heritage, an appointed body established in 1983 to manage government-owned archaeological sites. The surrounding area was bought up after a national fundraiser in the 1920s and given to the National Trust, an independent non-profit dedicated to land preservation. Currently, the Trust owns 827 hectares around the site, including numerous smaller archaeological sites.[25] Hence, unlike nearby Avebury Circle, there has never been significant modern settlement in or around the site, ensuring it has retained a rural character.

Of course, that's not to say the site remained a dormant place. With the rise of alternative religions, neo-paganism, the counterculture, and the rock and roll music scene, Stonehenge has continued to play a role not simply as a "historic site" but as a place where modern events occur. Moreover, folklore continues to arise about the site, such as those who have attributed it to the work of extraterrestrials based off of the writings of Erich von Däniken.[26] Others believe that Stonehenge is connected to avenues of spiritual power called "Ley Lines" that criss-cross Britain.

Given the mysteries, the history, and the debates, it is no surprise that Stonehenge is perhaps the most controversial, protested, and disputed ancient monument in the world today. None of

---

25 "Stonehenge Landscape: Visitor Information." Accessed online at: http://www.nationaltrust.org.uk/stonehenge-landscape/
26 *Chariots of the Gods* (1968)

the issues of primary importance — its original purpose, its owners, its contemporary meaning, and what is needed for its conservation — have been answered by anything approaching a scholarly consensus. Every year, it is the site of an "annual summer solstice ritual of confrontation between forces of order and disorder"[27]. Much of this confrontation is due to the fact that the site has immense spiritual and symbolic importance for a broad population of druids, neo-pagans, New Age Travellers, and other members of Britain's "counterculture."

Picture of a Druid initiation ritual at Stonehenge in 1905

Much of the tension is due to the fact that for the official guardians and interpreters of Stonehenge — English Heritage, the National Trust, English Nature and the archaeological community — Stonehenge is fundamentally a place of the past and a piece of Britain's "heritage." However, for those countercultural groups, Stonehenge is far from dead and cold; it is, in the words of cultural historian Andy Worthington, a "living temple" and an "icon of alternative Britain".

The focal point of this confrontation has always been the visually dramatic events that occur during the summer and winter solstices, especially the dawn alignments at the summer solstice, which many Britons have found to be the perfect time for a night-long celebration of life and love. These rituals, invented in the 18th century, are the product of a religious and social movement called Druidism or, to contrast it with its pre-Roman inspiration: Neo-Druidism.

The Druid's (or Gorsedd) Prayer
Original by Iolo Morganwg

27 From Christopher Chippindale's review of Andy Worthington's *Stonehenge: Celebration and Subversion* (2004)

This Version by the Order of Bards, Ovates and Druids

"Grant, O Holy Ones, Thy Protection;
And in protection, strength;
And in strength, understanding;
And in understanding, knowledge;
And in knowledge, the knowledge of justice;
And in the knowledge of justice, the love of it;
And in that love, the love of all existences;
And in the love of all existences the love of Earth our mother and all goodness."

Stonehenge, and stone monuments like it around Britain, have been indefinably linked in the minds of the people of Britain with the "druids" since the writings of the 18th century archaeologist William Stukeley. Stukeley, however, did not act alone; around Britain, upper class (often Anglican) Britons were at this time seeking to understand the ancient "Celtic" religions of their islands. For many, the druids held a great attraction, and the people began to form Druidic Orders around the writings of scholars like Stukeley and Iolo Morganwg (1747-1826). Morganwg, a Welsh nationalist, claimed to have found documents detailing druidic rituals, and even though it is now known that he faked the original documents, his ceremonials have made a deep impact upon the modern Druidic Movement. A variation of his ritual is still performed yearly at Stonehenge.

The work of writers like Morganwg was aided by the nature of the site. 19th century romantics were often caught up in the Salisbury Plain's barren, rugged and windswept nature. They popularized the concept of the "sublime," a natural landscape with the power to inspire the fear of God into the visitor, and this was contrasted with the "beautiful" landscapes that represented the pleasant and soft side of nature. 19th century visitors to Stonehenge came not so much to wonder about historic facts but to shiver at the barbarity of the ancient Britons and the sublime terror of the monument of the landscape. For those who could not visit the site personally, it was further popularized by the paintings of Romantic artists like J.M.W. Turner, and John Constable, who depicted a ruinous, eerie landscape. This experience was understood as a fundamentally religious and aesthetic one, and it has served to undergird the spiritual encounter between the neo-druids and the monument. While early archaeologists may have shared this sense, today it fundamentally separates the religious and scientific connections people have with the site.

Constable's painting of Stonehenge (1835)

Turner's painting of Stonehenge (1828)

The modern druid movement has bifurcated into two branches. On the one hand, there is the Gorseddau, which are ceremonial institutions in Wales, Cornwall and the continental region of

Brittany that aim to promote their local Celtic cultures and languages (Welsh, Cornish and Breton respectively) within the context of yearly rituals and awards ceremony. The events are something of a mix of a Masonic ceremony, the Celtic Oscars, and the Queen's yearly nomination of knighthoods. These ceremonies are traditionally associated strongly with stone circles. For instance, the first Cornish Gorsedd (the singular of Gorseddau) was held in 1928 in the stone circle of Boscawen Un, and the much-larger Welsh Gorseth now uses custom-built stone circles for its events.[28] Morganwg's rituals consciously integrated these circles, making them sacred ground which only the members of the Gorsedd, the initiated bards, ovates and druids, could enter.

However, while Stonehenge was perhaps the model that Morganwg had in mind in the 1780s, it is not located within a traditional Celtic country. It is located directly within the thoroughly English county of Wiltshire, and thus it has never been the site of a nationalist Gorsedd ceremony. Instead, it has been adopted by the other strand of the Druid tradition: the religious neo-pagans. For these individuals, the Celtic languages are not crucial. Instead, they seek to reconstruct the ancient pre-Christian sun worshipping religion of the islands. Druidism in this form is a highly dualistic religion, contrasting the male sun with the female moon, rationality with irrationality, light with dark.[29]

The ceremony performed yearly in Stonehenge at the solstice is done by the Glastonbury Order of Druids and their political wing, the Loyal Arthurian Warband. The members of the Order dress in ritual robes and process into the circle. They perform a ritual based upon Morganwg's original. They enter the sacred circle and "call" to the four cardinal directions, blowing a ram's horn and chanting the ritual question "is there peace?" The ritual then involves the invocation of the Druid's Prayer, written by Morganwg and used by both Gorseddau and Neo-Druids, and the prayers and ceremonial continues until the climax: the rising of the sun over the Heelstone. The druids perform a second rite at noon, and then the sacred circle is "opened", which means the non-initiated public is allowed in. Since the time of the Free Festivals, members of the New Age Traveller community enter and perform marriages and baby naming ceremonies, scatter the ashes of their dead, and generally commune with the stones and one another.[30]

This ritual tradition (and the accompanying yearly crowds of spectators) was mostly unchanged throughout the first 70 years of the 20th century. However, by the 1970s, there was a

---

28 "The Gorsedd Stone Circle" at the Museum of Wales homepage. Accessed online at: http://www.museumwales.ac.uk/cy/902/

29 *Blood and Mistletoe: The History of the Druids in Britain* (2011) and *Triumph of the Moon: A History of Modern Pagan Witchcraft* both by Ronald Hutton (1999) published by Yale University Press and Oxford University Press respectively are perhaps the best social histories of modern neo-paganism in Britain. Hutton is one of the few scholars respected by both historians (he is a Reader at Oxford and a Commissioner of English Heritage) and neo-pagans (whose defense he has come to numerous times).

30 For a blow-by-blow description of a similar Gorsedd ceremony, visit the "Open Gorseth" page of the Gorseth Kernow: http://www.gorsethkernow.org.uk/english/ceremony.htm. For the website of the Order, visit: http://www.glastonburyorderofdruids.com/

growing interest in the site amongst those involved in alternative "New Age" religions, and many saw it as the paragon of ancient holy places. These people, many of them branded "hippies" by the press, began to also arrive at Stonehenge starting in the mid-1970s and started a new tradition: the Stonehenge Free Festival.

The tradition of summer festivals at Stonehenge is actually far older than the Stonehenge Free Festival, with the first recorded one in 1680 and the first on Midsummer on 1781. In the 19th century, there were legal challenges over the right of the landowner to fence the site and to charge entry and deny festivals. The discovery of the alignment and the growth of neo-Druidry has meant that the site was used for religious ceremonies by Druidic groups since the 1920s. With the druidic ceremonies inevitably came crowds of curious onlookers.[31]

This scene evolved further from 1974-1984 with the appearance of the Free Festival, growing out of a New Age interest in the site. Initially, groups of itinerant pagans began to camp out on nearby fields, having a festival that culminated during the solstice, but the events grew quickly in size. Eventually, there was an annual gathering for a national community of "New Age Travellers" who wandered Britain in small convoys. In addition to its religious character, Stonehenge became a central event of their yearly calendar for the Travellers, offering a chance to gather as a community. As a "free festival," however, there was no admission charged and no governing authority. As the archaeologist and historian Christopher Chippendale noted, it was a "time when the Lord of Misrule governs", and for them the site was not "a dry agnostic relic to be dissected by academic archaeologists, but a sacred place of living powers". Even as early as 1978, the Travellers criticized the official custodians' care, including the existence of a road that splits the henge from the avenue, the large paved parking lot, the decaying visitors' facilities, the barbed wire, and the arc lamps.

There was, however, also a growing presence of drugs. In 1982, an organized street of tents openly sold controlled substances with posted prices. By 1983, the festival grew to six weeks in length and included up to 30,000 participants. Naturally, the size and length of the festival caused damage to the surrounding countryside.[32] That same year, the government merged a number of previous institutions – the Ancient Monuments Board for England, the Historic Buildings Council for England and the monuments division of the Department of the Environment – to create the semi-autonomous English Heritage. The question of the Stonehenge Free Festival quickly became the institution's first major challenge, and the new Commissioners would respond strongly.

---

31 "Stoned Henge: Events and Issues at the Summer Solstice 1985" by Christopher Chippendale in the journal *World Archaeology* no 18 (1), pp 38-59 (1985) pg 42
32 "Stoned Henge: Events and Issues at the Summer Solstice 1985" by Christopher Chippendale in the journal *World Archaeology* no 18 (1), pp 38-59 (1985)

Picture of the Stonehenge Free Festival in 1984

By 1985, English Heritage – supported by Wiltshire County Council – banned all gatherings, including the separate Druidic ceremonies, at the site. They sent out thousands of posters, gained the power to close roads, and put out new razor wire restraints around the site. Proposals by Traveller groups for alternative festival sites near the area were rejected. This set the stage for a confrontation that would serve as the most important event in the site's 20th century history.[33]

In June 1985, Margaret Thatcher's government had an "exclusion zone" on the Summer Solstice for four miles on all sides around Stonehenge, banning all visitors, but a group of New Age Travellers called "The Convoy" attempted to challenge the exclusion zone. The Convoy consisted of somewhere between 80 and 120 vehicles and over 700 individuals. The group approached the henge en-masse but were blocked by mounds of gravel on the road. The halted procession was then attacked by the police, 1,600 of whom had been gathered for the event and who used billy clubs to smash windshields. Most of the group fled into a nearby beanfield, where they were surrounded. Attempts to negotiate a retreat were turned down by the police, and a several-hour standoff ensued. Throughout the standoff, several Convoy members were assaulted and taken away, primarily with head injuries, by ambulance. When riot police arrived, the Convoy members attempted to flee – some in their vehicles – and were followed and attacked by the police. The ensuing events are still disputed, but Convoy members claim that police assaulted them with rocks, fire extinguishers and riot gear. Overall, over 700 Travellers were arrested, the single largest arrest in British history to that point.[34]

---

33 "Stoned Henge: Events and Issues at the Summer Solstice 1985" by Christopher Chippendale in the journal
  World Archaeology no 18 (1), pp 38-59 (1985)
34 Varying accounts of the events can be found in: *Battle of the Beanfield* by Andy Worthington (2005) Enabler

Thatcher had little love for the New Age Travellers, reportedly calling them "a horde of medieval brigands", and both Thatcher and her successor (fellow Conservative John Major) sought to repress their movement. The government denied them campsites, tracked their movements, and arrested them throughout the countryside.[35] Ironically, studies of Traveller populations found that many were unemployed or homeless in 1985 as a direct result of Thatcher's restructuring and de-industrializing of the British economy. It appears that the repression at the Beanfield was only the first blow in this larger campaign aimed at criminalizing their lifestyle and any large-scale protest or alternative gathering.

In the immediate post-Beanfield period, there was an attempt to emphasize the need to "protect" Stonehenge. For instance, the 1985 documentary "Who Built Stonehenge?" for the BBC's show *Horizon* opened with this description: "It's a magnet for visitors from all over the world. Each year, three-quarters of a million people come to see it. They're prepared to pay for the privilege of staring at a ruin. To preserve what's left, they're not allowed to enter and are kept at a distance. […] in order to protect the monument, for the past two years [the Neo-Druids] have been banned from holding their ceremony along with the hippies who regard Stonehenge as their cathedral of love and peace."

As late as 1997, an American documentary for the PBS series NOVA (1997) took an even stronger stand: "In the 20th century, a modern cult of Druids adopted the temple as their own and used it as a stage for elaborate solstice ceremonies. But in the 1970s and 80s their pagan services were gradually overwhelmed by hippies, drugs and the international press. To protect the monument, British authorities now close Stonehenge on the summer solstice."

Today, the summer solstice celebrations once again bring in thousands of spectators. These events have recently seen crowds of 14,500 (in 2012) and 18,000 (2011), despite rain on both dates.[36] While there is certainly a religious contingent present, with some revelers pressing themselves up against the stones to absorb their healing energies and others performing elaborate Druidic rituals (including two marriages in 2011), much of the celebration can be better understood as an ecstatic celebration of life. The events abound with colorful costumes, feathers, flowers and eccentric musical orchestration (for instance, a jam session made up of conga drums, tuba, flute and a ram's horn).[37] While the body of the Peace Convoy may have been shattered,

Publications; "Stoned Henge: Events and Issues at the Summer Solstice 1985" by Christopher Chippendale in the journal *World Archaeology* no 18 (1), pp 38-59 (1985); "A Criminal Culture?" by Jim Carey, accessed online at http://dreamflesh.com/essays/crimculture/ ; "On This Day, June 1st 1985: Hippies Clash With Police at Stonehenge" http://news.bbc.co.uk/onthisday/hi/dates/stories/june/1/newsid_2493000/2493267.stm;

35 "For New Age Travellers, the End of the Road?" by John Darton, 13 Apr 1994 in *The Bristol Journal*. Accessed online at: http://www.nytimes.com/1994/04/13/world/bristol-journal-for-new-age-travelers-the-end-of-the-road.html

36 "Solstice Revellers Celebrate Grey and West Midsummer Dawn at Stonehenge" *The Telegraph* July 6th, 2012 and "Traditional British Downpour for Ancient Stonehenge Midsummer Rituals" in *The Telegraph* by John Bingham, June 21st, 2011.

37 Bingham, 2011

the spirit that animated the Travellers in the 1970s and 80s continues.

One of the animating spirits, and a personification of the contemporary culture swirling around the stones, is Arthur Uther Pendragon. Formerly named John Rothwell, Pendragon (born in 1958) was a participant in the pre-Beanfield Free Festivals as a member of a motorcycle gang. He changed his name officially in 1986, soon after Thatcher's repression of the Free Festivals. He, along with the political wing of the Glastonbury Order of Druids, became a focal point of protest of the stones, by participating in and giving magical support to environmental protests throughout Britain.[38] Their greatest success came when Pendragon challenged English Heritage's ban on Solstice festivals at the European Court of Human Rights once in 1998 and then again in 2009.[39]

The late 20th century events at Stonehenge also led to transformations within the Neo-Druidic movement. The old druidry was associated with elderly Anglicans and Celtic nationalists, but the new Druidry came to embrace the spirit of the Free Festival and the "Lord of Misrule." Organizations like the Secular Order of Druids, the Loyal Arthurian Warband and the Glastonbury Order of Druids were organized in the late 1980s in order to directly challenge the governmental actions that caused the Beanfield: English Heritage, the police, the County Government and the Conservative Powers-that-Be in Parliament. They became protest groups, using the struggle for Stonehenge as a rallying point and barometer for their wider movements for ecology, nuclear disarmament, and a return to what they envision as pre-Christian values.[40] Even today, they remain prominent elements of the British druidic community)

Chapter 4: Tourism and Context

For most people, Stonehenge is neither a place of academic research nor a site of religious ecstasy. For most, it is a historic site and a potential tourist attraction. For decades, hundreds of thousands of visitors have made the trek onto the Salisbury Plain each year, making Stonehenge one of the most popular destinations in all of Britain.

Despite its rural isolation, Stonehenge is a relatively easy place to visit and is immensely popular. Most visitors come by car, arriving along the A3028 west from Andover or east from Warminster. There is parking on the site, but people can also come by public transport via the Salisbury train station or take the local buses to the site. More adventurous tourists use the National Cycle Network or hike, as it is a comfortable two mile stroll from Amesbury.

---

38 "The Raving Outlaw Biker-Druids and Their 1575-Year-Old King." by Matt Shea accessed online at http://www.vice.com/read/all-hail-king-arthur-uther-pendragon
39 "Stonehenge protester King Arthur Pendragon defies eviction order" in *The Guardian* May 3rd, 2009
40 For an example of this shift, one would do well to read the eulogies for Tim Sebastion, the founder of the Secular Order of Druids who played a crucial role in changing the face of modern druidry directly in response to the Battle of the Beanfield: http://www.grahamharvey.org/Tim.htm and http://wildhunt.org/2007/02/remembering-chief-druid.html

Many contemporary visitors often have a mixed reaction to the site, something that almost all commentators (including English Heritage) recognize. It is undoubtedly an impressive monument, but the site lies along the side of route A344, which actually cuts over the top of the ceremonial Avenue (where the sun rises on the summer solstice) and almost as close to the A304. Many visitors are shocked to see the site come into view while driving and are often turned off by the presence of fences around the perimeter. The visitor's center is equally disappointing. A decaying 1960s pre-fabricated building, it leads to a concrete tunnel under the A344 before arriving at the site. There is also no question that while everyone knows a little bit about Stonehenge, many are surprised that the structure is not nearly as big as they imagined.

Despite that, there are changes in the air. After decades of complaints by heritage officials, archaeologists, druid groups and uncounted tourists, English Heritage has launched a plan for 2013-14 to completely renovate the site. The plan, which has a budget of £27 million, includes the removal of the A344, the construction of a new visitor center, and the reversion of hundreds of hectares of surrounding land into fence-less chalk plains to resemble the neolithic landscape. Plans are also afoot to construct a recreation of a neolithic village based on nearby archaeological digs and to allow visitors to approach the site along the Avenue, as was originally intended by the builders thousands of years ago.[41] For many, these plans cannot come soon enough, as there is a growing consensus that Stonehenge, which should be the crown jewel of British Heritage, is one of the nation's greatest embarrassments.[42]

Even for those who cannot visit the original Stonehenge, all is not lost because Stonehenge has reached the cultural state of a true global icon. It is instantly recognizable, and it has been referenced, copied, mocked and depicted thousands of times. Its mere image invokes ideas about ancient mystery, druidic rites, and neolithic genius. As a result, Stonehenge can be a symbol exported to other contexts. The most amusing of these are the faux-henges: Carhenge (a replica built in the Nebraska cornfields out of old Buicks in 1987), Foamhenge (a "perfect" replica made out of foam in Virginia), Twinkiehenge (built at the 2001 Burning Man Festival out of the famous pre-packaged dessert), Tankhenge (in post-Berlin Wall Berlin out of Soviet personnel carriers) and the unnamed replica by famous street artist Banksy made with portable toilets at the 2007 Glastonbury Festival. Then there are the Stonehenge astronomical references: Manhattanhenge (the name for the day when the sun rises or sets along the east-west avenues of Manhattan, much as it does through the stones of the henge) and MITHenge (a similar phenomenon on a long hallway in the Massachusetts Institute of Technology). It even has seen

---

41 "Stonehenge Gets a £27m facelift to end 'national embarrassment'" by Steve Morris in *The Guardian*, 11 July 2012 Accessed online at: http://www.guardian.co.uk/culture/2012/jul/11/stonehenge-facelift-a344-english-heritage

42 "Disgrace of the Squalid Mess Around Stonehenge" Letter to the Editor of *The Telegraph* from Sir Angus Stirling 11 May 2011 (http://www.telegraph.co.uk/comment/letters/8505501/Disgrace-of-the-squalid-mess-around-Stonehenge.html); "Stonehenge: Road to Ruin" by Charles Spencer in *The Telegraph*, 9 May 2011 (http://www.telegraph.co.uk/culture/8498869/Stonehenge-road-to-ruin.html);

use in the heavy metal scene thanks to Black Sabbath, which toured with a replica in 1983-4, and Stonehenge lent its name to a World War II submarine that disappeared in the Pacific in 1943.

There is no question that Stonehenge is the greatest megalithic site in all of Britain, and that its surrounding landscape may turn out to be one the best preserved testaments to Britain's neolithic peoples. However, megalithic construction is not limited to Stonehenge or even Britain; it is a characteristic of the entire Atlantic Coast of Europe, and similar constructions can be found in other areas of the world. The European megalithic cultures built numerous styles of buildings: from Irish court tombs to Cornish quoits, mesolithic tombs of Scandinavia and even the Skorba tombs of Malta. Beyond Europe, similar traditions can be found in places as widely scattered as Easter Island, Northern China and Yemen.

Outside of Stonehenge, perhaps the best-known and most important megalithic monument is the henge at Avebury. Located less than 20 miles from Stonehenge, it was constructed of similar sarsens and probably predates the more famous site. Avebury is notable because it is the largest stone circle in Britain at over 1,000 feet in diameter. In fact, the village of Avebury was built into the circle itself, sometimes incorporating the rough-hewn stones into the walls of the houses. Like Stonehenge, it has an "avenue" of approach (the "Kennet Avenue") and associated nearby sites: the West Kennet Long Barrow and Silbury Hill, a 125 foot high artificial hill, both of which predate Avebury itself. Avebury is popular with many visitors because of the lack of restrictions over the site. Visitors can move amongst the stones, touch them, leave offerings, and pose for pictures.

Avebury Henge and Village

The stone circle phenomenon – the "Henge" – is found throughout Britain. The word "Henge" originates in Stonehenge and was retroactively applied to similar constructions elsewhere. Some of the more famous sites include the Thornborough Henges in Yorkshire, which is made up of three identical connected henges aligned in a row, the Ring of Brodgar on the island of Orkney, and Boscawen-un and the Merry Maidens (two circles in sight of one another) in Cornwall.

Aerial view of Thornborough's three henges

Brittany, today a peninsula controlled by France, has long had strong cultural connections with the Celtic peoples of southern Britain and is home to a large concentration of megaliths, including the Broken Menhir of Er Grah at the village of Locmariaquer. It was at one time the largest stone erected by pre-historic peoples, standing over 60 feet tall and weighing 254 tons. In comparison, Stonehenge used sarsen stones that were closer to 12 feet and 25 tons for the outer ring and 20 feet for the Great Trilithon. Spread over a vast period of time and space, these sites were most likely built by different cultural groups, but they obviously share a common architectural history and possibly theological rationale. For now, that history and purpose remain unclear.

The Broken Menhir of Er Grah

Outside of Europe, there are several rich Megalithic traditions. The Near East is home to standing stones and megalithic tombs along a broad band, stretching north from Yemen into Jordan, Syria, Israel, Lebanon and Turkey. An especially dense area for standing stones is the Golan Heights, along the border of Israel and Syria. Another distinct large-stone construction tradition existed in what is now northeastern China and the Korean Peninsula. Even further south, a megalithic tradition existed in some areas of Indonesia until the 20th century, especially on the island of Nias.[43] Some argue that the famous Moai statues of Easter Island should be considered megaliths, as they certainly meet the qualifications for size. The Moai in particular have inspired as much mystery and experimental archaeology as Stonehenge, with similar debates about the how, when, why and who of the builders.

Conclusion

"Pile of Stone-henge! so proud to hint yet keep
Thy secrets, thou that lov'st to stand and hear
The Plain resounding to the whirlwind's sweep,
Inmate of lonesome Nature's endless year."

As this excerpt from William Wordsworth's 1793 poem "Guilt and sorrow; or incidents upon Salisbury Plain," indicates, Stonehenge has captured people's imaginations for generations. To some extent, that task seems simple, since Stonehenge is a spectacular prehistoric monument, a

---

43 *Megalithic Traditions in Nias Island* by Lucas Partanda Koestoro and Ketut Wiradnyana (2007). Published by UNESCO. Accessed online at: http://unesdoc.unesco.org/images/0015/001517/151795eo.pdf

world heritage site, and a sacred place. However, so many questions remain about the builders: their identity, their lifestyles, their purpose in building the monument and the methods they used. While archaeology has increasingly provided insight into many of these questions, probably more than anyone would have predicted even a few decades ago, it still seems safe to assert that we will never know everything there is to know about Stonehenge. But in a sense, the layers of mystery and uncertainty only add to the allure of the site. At the same time, the notion that Stonehenge is a "living temple" helps explain why some people's fascination with Stonehenge has nothing to do with the newest discoveries by ground-penetrating radar.

While much of the 20th century's history of the site has been a story of confrontation, accusation and exclusion, the tides appear to be slowly shifting. While the era of six-week Free Festivals is probably over forever, the hippies and druids have returned for their Solstice celebrations. At times, scientists and pagans have worked together. As early as 1986, archaeologist Christopher Chippindale called for a detente and a soft approach to negotiations, and today many neo-pagans are deeply interested in what archaeologists have to do. They follow the ongoing developments in excavation, debate over what is to be done with excavated bodies, and even volunteer for digs and experimental archaeology projects.

In general, all signs point to things only getting better at Stonehenge in the years to come. Religious ceremonies and raucous festivals have found a place alongside serious scholarship and wide-eyed tourism. New archaeological finds, like the two nearby henges and the neolithic settlement at Durrington Walls, promise to broaden current knowledge about the neolithic builders and their beliefs, while also holding out the potential for future discoveries.

Finally, the site is being given the respect it deserves. The road bisecting it is disappearing, the chalk grasslands are being restored, and a proper visitor center with an accompanying museum and reconstructed village will be built. It has been a spectacular century of research, celebration and confrontation, and through it all the stones have stood as silent witness. With the exception of the neolithic era of the builders, there has perhaps never been a better time to visit or understand Stonehenge.

Bibliography

Bender, B, *Stonehenge: Making Space* (Berg Publishers, 1998)

Burl, A, *Great Stone Circles* (Yale University Press, 1999)

Chippindale, C, *Stonehenge Complete* (Thames and Hudson, London, 2004)

Cunliffe, B, & Renfrew, C, *Science and Stonehenge* (The British Academy 92, Oxford University Press, 1997)

John, Brian, *"The Bluestone Enigma: Stonehenge, Preseli and the Ice Age"* (Greencroft Books,

2008)

Johnson, Anthony, *Solving Stonehenge: The New Key to an Ancient Enigma* (Thames & Hudson, 2008)

North, J, Stonehenge: *Ritual Origins and Astronomy* (HarperCollins, 1997)

Pitts, M, Hengeworld (Arrow, London, 2001)

The Sphinx

The Great Sphinx of Giza

Chapter 1: The Riddle of the Sphinx

The mythology of the creature known as the Sphinx is as well known today as it was in the ancient world. A strange creature with the body of a lion and the head of a human, it features prominently in the story of Oedipus in Greek mythology, as depicted by Sophocles in the 429 B.C. play Oedipus Rex. The most common version of the story tells of how Hera, wife to Zeus and chief matriarchal figure amongst the Greek pantheon, ordered the Sphinx to leave her homeland in Ethiopia and journey to Thebes in Greece.

The Sphinx in the Greek tradition was a female creature, her human face looking out from atop the body of a lion, adorned by the wings of a great bird, unfolding and stretching upon her leonine back. Once settled by the roadside outside the gates of Thebes it was the task of the Sphinx to test travellers by asking them riddles. Those who could answer correctly were allowed to pass on into the city, while those who failed the test were condemned to die, devoured in the jaws of the great mythological beast. For a time it seemed that none could best the creature, her riddles unable to be solved, and the gateway to Thebes remained impassable to travellers, but that all changed when the Greek hero Oedipus arrived. He strode down the road, a masterful man of powerful visage, his footsteps sure as he made his way resolutely toward his destination. He could see the gates of Thebes ahead, his destination within reach, but it was then that the vast and terrible creature that rested by the roadside reared up beside him. The Sphinx made her challenge clear but Oedipus was unshaken in his resolve. Defiantly he stood ready, waiting for her questions, ready to answer.[44] The malevolent face of the Sphinx smiled as she boomed out her first riddle:

"There walks on land a creature of two feet, of four feet, and of three; it has one voice, but, sole among the animals that grow on land or in the sky or beneath the sea, it change its nature; nay, when it walks propped on most feet, then is the speed in its limbs less than it has ever been before."

"Man," Oedipus replied confidently, "in infancy creeping, in maturity erect, in old age walking feebly with a staff."[45]

Undaunted, the Sphinx continued with her second riddle, demanding to know: "There are two sisters: one gives birth to the other and she, in turn, gives birth to the first. Who are the two sisters?"

"They are day," Oedipus answered, "and they are night." Both times he had answered correctly, something that none had managed to do before. Frustrated and defeated, the Sphinx set upon herself in fury, tearing at her own body, devouring herself until there was nothing left. In other versions of the tale she climbed to a high place and threw herself down, breaking her body asunder upon the sharp and jagged rocks below.[46] The old ways of the Sphinx had been destroyed and the road to Thebes was clear once more, clear for the new Olympian gods, as represented in this story by the hero Oedipus.

The story of the Sphinx's riddle is about the old being supplanted by the new, and as much as it is a part of Greek mythology, it is made very clear that the Sphinx is not a member of the Greek pantheon of gods. Rather, it is something older and stranger, a final relic of an ancient and distant land. The etymology of the word "sphinx" bears the story of Greek intention in it as well. A Greek word, it either derives from the verb meaning "to squeeze" or is a Greek corruption of the Egyptian name "shesepankh", meaning "living image". Either way, the origin of the mythological creature points to Egypt, the word referring to the image of a statue there, having

---

[44] Sophocles. 1991. *Oedipus Rex*. Dover Thrift Editions, Dover Publications, USA.
[45] Athenaeus. 1930. *The Deipnosophistae of Athenaeus*. Loeb Classical Library edition, Harvard University Press, USA. pp 569.
[46] Science Dump. 2012. *The Riddle of the Sphinx*. Site accessed 28 June 2013. http://www.sciencedump.com/content/riddle-sphinx

been carved from a single stone, an image squeezed from the living rock. At least, this is the interpretation presented by historian Susan Bauer,[47] who points to the origin of the myth being the monumental statue which remains today one of the most famous images of the ancient world – the Great Sphinx of Giza.

Naturally, the Egyptians who carved the statue would not have used the word Sphinx to describe it, as the mythology of Egypt was very different from that which would develop around the changing iconography of later cultures and eras. The Great Sphinx of Giza for the Egyptians who carved it was part of a tradition of protective sentries, carved to watch over the tombs of the dead. Guardian statues were usually associated with the sun god Re and often had the image of the current pharaoh carved into them. It is for this reason that most scholars have long assumed the Sphinx's face represented the ruler who oversaw its construction.

As such, there are examples of both male and female sphinxes being produced in ancient Egypt. The Pharaoh Hatshepsut had her likeness carved upon numerous sphinx bodies, and her granite and alabaster statues are currently held in the permanent collections of museums from New York to Memphis. In Thebes, approximately 900 sphinxes were carved with ram heads to honor the god Amon. Sphinx statues came to feature atop stairwells in complexes, along avenues leading to temples and outside of tombs.[48]

[47] Bauer, S. Wise. 2007. *The History of the Ancient World*. W. W. Norton & Company Inc, New York. pp 110–112.
[48] Bodsworth, Jon. 2011. *Egypt Archive*. http://www.egyptarchive.co.uk

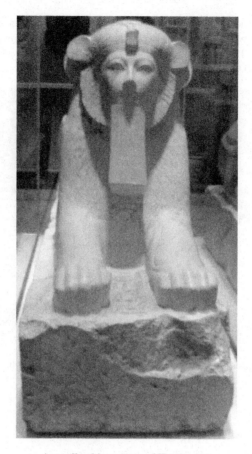

A small sphinx statue of Hatshepsut

The earliest version of the creature that would come to be known as the Sphinx has been attributed to Hetepheres II and dated to around the fourth dynasty of Egypt. Currently held in the permanent collection of the Cairo Museum in Egypt, this statue was composed of painted limestone and found at the site of the pyramid of Pharaoh Redjedef (or Djedefre) at Abu Rawash. The physical likeness was based on Hetepheres II, who was both half-sister and wife to the Pharaoh Redjedef (Djedefre), thought to be the successor of Pharaoh Khufu and predecessor to Pharaoh Khafre (his younger brother).[49] What the origin was of this design, of a lion body with the head of a human, is unknown, but it would come to be a recurring motif that proliferated out

[49] Bodsworth, Jon. 2011. *Egypt Archive*. http://www.egyptarchive.co.uk

of Egypt and spread across multiple other cultures around the world. There was even a winged Sphinx located on a wall frieze at the palace of Darius the Great, ruler of the Persian Empire. That version depicted a lion body, bearded male face and wings, located at Susa and dating to approximately 480 B.C.

Scholars believe this is a Sphinx statue of Hetepheres II that dates back to the 4th Dynasty (circa 2723-2563 B.C.)

An ancient Persian wall carving depicting a winged Sphinx from the palace of Darius the Great

Ancient Greek marble statue of a sphinx from the 6th century B.C.

An Indian sphinx that stands guard at the entrance of the Shri Shiva Nataraja temple

Chapter 2: Construction and Reconstruction

The Sphinx continues to be a recurring motif in imagery of the past and is utilized regularly to this day. Its replication on stamps, coins and other such nationalistic documentation for Egypt however, has more to do with one Sphinx in particular: the monumental statue located near Cairo that stands as such a poignant illustration of the ancient world. Of all the sphinxes throughout Egypt, the most famous of all was and is the Great Sphinx of Giza, a monumental statue that has become a renowned part of the landscape of Egypt's past and present, positioned as it is before the line of pyramids that stretch off into the desert. This Sphinx, unlike the Greek mythological version, has the face of a man rather than a woman. To trace the reasons for this however, one must look not to the stories of Greek mythology but to the history and archaeology of ancient Egypt.

The Great Sphinx of Giza is located on the Giza Plateau on the Nile's western bank, near Cairo. It is placed next to the Great Pyramid of Giza, below the pyramids, facing toward the east. The date of construction for this iconic feature remains a debated topic in contemporary Egyptology, but the most accepted period for construction is cited as during the reign of the Pharaoh Khafre, whose face it is reasoned was used as the basis for the physical features of the Sphinx's own face. Although this is still debated, the evidence used to justify it includes the placement of Khafre's own tomb, close to the Great Sphinx, and that computer reconstructions of the face of the monument align with other images of Khafre found in the archaeological record.[50]

Panorama of the Sphinx with the Great Pyramid at Giza in the background

As befitted a culture whose religious focus was on the afterlife, funerary customs expanded in complexity and ceremony just as the houses for the dead became monumental features of the landscape, serving as veritable mansions for the beloved departed. The greatest of these structures were to be the province of the richest and most powerful – the rulers of Egypt themselves. The Great Pyramid of Giza is perhaps the best known of all these monuments, a mountain of stone built upon the west bank of the Nile to house the mortal remains of the Pharaoh Khufu. It is estimated that this structure, one of the Seven Wonders of the Ancient World, was commissioned by the pharaoh around 2575 B.C, early on during his 23 year reign. The work was so great that it absorbed much of Khufu's period as pharaoh to see it completed. With approximately 2,300,000 stone blocks of roughly 2,500 kilograms, each laid out in a geometrically precise design, it is a stunning piece of monumental architecture and an outstanding technical building achievement. It is important to note however, that the pyramid as it looks in present day was not how it looked upon completion at the end of Khufu's reign. At that time, limestone blocks were used to form its outer edges, meaning that it would have shone brightly in the light of the sun, a dazzling reminder after internment of the great pharaoh so recently departed.[51]

---

[50] Papanek, John (editor). 1992. *Egypt: Land of the Pharaohs.* Time Life Books, USA. pp 66-67.

The next pharaoh was Khufu's son Khafre (also spelt Khafra, Khefren or even Chephren in the Greek tradition), who followed his father's example in building a pyramid for his own mortal remains. Khafre also created something unique in that landscape of Egypt that no other pharaoh had done before or would do after. It is believed that during the building of the Great Pyramid of Giza all local rock outcrops would have been utilized as sources of raw materials for manufacture. Nearby both the Great Pyramid of Giza and the location of Khafre's own chosen resting place was a remnant outcrop, left over from the work of stonecutters busily scouring the landscape to create suitable building materials for the monumental works ordered by the pharaoh.

However, rather than have it utilized for further stone blocks, Khafre had another idea altogether. He ordered that the outcrop be reshaped into the embodiment of a mythical creature. In the years that followed, the tradition would continue to develop in ancient Egypt for devoting sculpted mythical guardians for sacred places. These guardians would be visualized as creatures with human faces and lion bodies. Such mythical beasts would be realized in varying forms and sizes throughout Egypt in association with tombs, but none would ever be so vast or grand as that sculpted from the outcrop on the orders of Pharaoh Khafre. Approximately 70 feet tall and 240 feet in length from outstretched paws to folded haunches, the face of this beast was probably fashioned into a likeness of the pharaoh himself. A later Egyptologist would hypothesize that the intention might have been to present an image of the Pharaoh Khafre transformed into the god Horus, presenting the sun god Re with offerings.[52] The Sphinx also had inscriptions that refer to the Egyptian lion god Ruri, who the Egyptians believed guarded the entrance to the underworld. Lehner has gone so far as to note the astronomical alignment of the Sphinx and the pyramid of Khafre during equinoxes, explaining, "At the very same moment, the shadow of the Sphinx and the shadow of the pyramid, both symbols of the king, become merged silhouettes. The Sphinx itself, it seems, symbolized the pharaoh presenting offerings to the sun god in the court of the temple." That said, as Egyptologist James Allen cautions, "The Egyptians didn't write history, so we have no solid evidence for what its builders thought the Sphinx was....Certainly something divine, presumably the image of a king, but beyond that is anyone's guess."

It has been estimated that the monument was first sculpted around 2500 B.C., and to this day, the great stone beast guards the Giza necropolis at its eastern approach, with further pyramids and monuments since added to the landscape, including those of Khafre and his wives.[53] The Pharaoh Khafre did not immediately succeed his father Khufu, but rather began his own reign after the short rule of the Pharaoh Redjedef (or Djedefre), generally interpreted as Khafre's elder brother. Pharaoh Khafre was the fourth pharaoh in the 4th dynasty, reigning between 2575 and 2465 B.C. He had at least four wives, according to the available written sources of his era,

---

[51] Time Life Books. 1987. *The Age of God-Kings*. Time Life Books Inc, USA.
[52] Lehner, Mark. 1985. *The Pyramid Tomb of Hetep-heres and the Satellite Pyramid of Khufu*. Mainz am Rhein, Germany.
[53] Zivie-Coche, Christiane. 2002. *Sphinx: History of a Monument*. Cornell University Press. pp 99–100.

including the queen Meresankh III as well as his own sister Khamerernebti. He also had numerous children, at least 12 sons and 4 daughters, with known names including Nebemakhet, Duaenre, Niuserre, Khentetka, Menkaure, Sekhemkare, Nikaure, Ankhmare, Akhre, Iunmin, Iunre, Shepsetkau, Rekhetre and Hemetre, drawn from inscriptions from tombs and temple walls.[54]

Not a great deal is known about Khafre or his reign, but his own pyramid demonstrates his influence and power, since it is almost as grand in size as the vast Great Pyramid of Giza attributed to his father Pharaoh Khufu. Other structures known to have been constructed during Khafre's reign include a valley temple linked to his pyramid via a causeway. The causeway was constructed from large blocks of granite, decorated along its extent by statuary carved from diorite quarried in the Nubian Desert.[55] In the later writings of the Greek historian Herodotus, Pharaoh Khafre was described as heretical, a cruel ruler who forced the Egyptian temples to stay closed after his father Pharaoh Khufu sealed them, but considering the gulf of time between Pharaoh Khafre's reign and the writings of Herodotus, however, those words must be considered for what they are, a secondary source passed down by word of mouth and fraught with possible errors and inconsistencies.[56]

[54] Dodson, Aidan & Hilton, Dyan. 2004. *The Complete Royal Families of Ancient Egypt*. Thames & Hudson.
[55] Encyclopædia Britannica. 2013. *Khafre*. Site accessed 14 July 2013.
    http://www.britannica.com/EBchecked/topic/316035/Khafre
[56] Herodotus (translated by Grene, David).1988. *Herodotus – The History*. University Of Chicago Press, USA.

Diorite statue of Khafre found in the Valley Temple

One of the overriding questions is who built the Sphinx. It was long assumed that laborers and/or slaves were used, but recent Egyptologists have unearthed the remains of a large settlement likely used to house the workers, and evidence from there suggests that the people working on the Sphinx were not from lower classes. In addition to the workers apparently being fed well, the settlement could hold up to 1500-2000 people at a time. Egyptologist Lehner has speculated that ordinary Egyptians did shifts of construction work, meaning that different people shuffled in and out of the area to work on the Sphinx. If so, this was a system similar to the one used over 4,000 years later by the Inca to build Machu Picchu.

The past was a vibrant, living landscape, and like the Great Pyramid of Giza, the Sphinx presumably ordered built by Khafre did not always appear then as it does now. The aesthetic of contemporary Egypt to the modern viewer is a familiar one in our current world. The crumbling sand blasted structures and raw sandstone blocks are an image tainted with nostalgia, evoking a poetic vision of the ancient past. The reality, however, is that the past was an environment with an aesthetic quite different from its archaeological remains. The broken nose of Khafre's Sphinx face was whole and full at one point, marks of weathering were absent, the statue may once have been adorned with a beard, and there is even evidence to suggest the monument was once painted in full color.

Limestone fragments of the Sphinx's beard

A number of attempts have been made to reconstruct how the Great Sphinx of Giza would have looked just after its completion, but with such limited available data, these attempts are more guesswork than science. Nevertheless, reconstructions are important in demonstrating how different the landscape of the past really was. American Egyptologist Mark Lehner is one heritage practitioner who has utilized modern technology to shed new light on the past. After measuring and planning the physical Sphinx, drawing it from multiple angles and photographing it with a stereoscopic camera, Lehner digitized a three dimensional model of it with the assistance of Egyptologist Ulrich Kapp, architect Thomas Jaggers and the German Archaeological Institute in Cairo. An image of Khafre was superimposed to fit over and fix the weatherworn and damaged face, the pedestal remnants between the outstretched legs of the Sphinx were altered to support a tall statue of Amenhotep II, and color was added across the surface of the Sphinx itself.[57] The available evidence for how the Sphinx may have been colored is very limited, with remnant residues of red pigment on the face, along with some traces of blue and yellow paint elsewhere. [58] While such reconstructions of the past may rely on a combination of guesswork and reason, the origin of the painted colors can at least be solved through the inscriptions of the past.

The colored facelift for the Sphinx occurred some 11 centuries after its initial construction, around 1400 B.C. The story of how and why this occurred was recorded on a granite stele placed between the outstretched paws of the Great Sphinx of Giza at the completion of the reconstruction works. The story recorded therein tells of the Pharaoh Thutmose IV, the son of Amenhotep II, who one day fell tired upon the Giza plateau and rested there, snoozing in the warm Egyptian afternoon sun. As he fell into a deep sleep, he saw in a dream the Sphinx come alive before him as a god, combining within it aspects of both the sun god Re and the god Horus. "You will be king," the Sphinx, or god combination Horemakhet as Thutmose IV thought of him, spoke in the dream. "You, Thutmose, will be king, but only if you free me! Free me from the shifting sands that bury my body in their flow, then you shall be granted power!"[59] When he woke from the dream, Thutmose IV had taken the words to heart and set about excavating the deep drifts of sand that had at that time settled around the body of the Sphinx. In addition to that, he encased the monument in limestone blocks and had it painted in the colors red, blue and yellow. He also erected a statue of his father Amenhotep II between the paws of the great stone beast and built a mud brick enclosure wall around the Great Sphinx of Giza, shaped to resemble a cartouche. Just as the dream had prophesied, Thutmose IV did indeed become the next Pharaoh of Egypt.[60]

The story of Thutmose IV's works was preserved on his stele, now known as the Dream Stele, part of which read, "... the royal son, Thothmos, being arrived, while walking at midday and

[57] Lehner, Mark. 1985. *The Pyramid Tomb of Hetep-heres and the Satellite Pyramid of Khufu*. Mainz am Rhein, Germany; Papanek, John (editor). 1992. *Egypt: Land of the Pharaohs*. Time Life Books, USA. pp 66-67.
[58] Hadingham, Evan. 2010. Riddle of the Sphinx. Cosmos Magazine. Site accessed 8 July 2013.
   http://www.cosmosmagazine.com/features/riddle-sphinx/
[59] Papanek, John (editor). 1992. *Egypt: Land of the Pharaohs*. Time Life Books, USA. pp 60-66.
[60] Papanek, John (editor). 1992. *Egypt: Land of the Pharaohs*. Time Life Books, USA. pp 60-66.

seating himself under the shadow of this mighty god, was overcome by slumber and slept at the very moment when Ra is at the summit. He found that the Majesty of this august god spoke to him with his own mouth, as a father speaks to his son, saying: Look upon me, contemplate me, O my son Thothmos; I am thy father, Harmakhis-Khopri-Ra-Tum; I bestow upon thee the sovereignty over my domain, the supremacy over the living ... Behold my actual condition that thou mayest protect all my perfect limbs. The sand of the desert whereon I am laid has covered me. Save me, causing all that is in my heart to be executed."

This was all added to further by other pharaohs who built a chapel around it, but in the end the sands returned, at times burying the paws and body of the Sphinx, at other times burying the vast monument completely. Nonetheless, the Sphinx peered out from the sands more often than not over the past few thousand years, sometimes appearing as just a head sticking out of the sand with its timeless eyes from the ancient past watching as the world continued to change around it. When early 20th century excavation finally succeeded in clearing away the sand from the base of the Sphinx, the *New York Times* itself reported, "The Sphinx has thus emerged into the landscape out of shadows of what seemed to be an impenetrable oblivion."

Chapter 3: Through the Ages

The building of a chapel around the stele of Thutmose IV has led Egyptologists to argue there may have been a Sphinx cult in existence during the Old Kingdom period of Egypt. While there is no specific evidence to support this, the presence of the chapel at the base of the Great Sphinx of Giza has suggested the possibility of religious use. There are, however, no records of priests servicing the Sphinx temple, which some have interpreted as never having been a completed structure. Either way, the monument itself was certainly popular during the Old Kingdom period, and other earlier structures were apparently harvested for use as raw material in the Sphinx's reconstruction and restoration. Ironically, the causeway of Khafre's pyramid was one casualty, as it was broken up to provide the stone to both repair the Sphinx and to build the temple in its honor.[61]

The image of the Sphinx even remained popular during the Amarna Period, a time when the traditional gods and religions of Egypt were forcibly abandoned on the orders of the Pharaoh Akhenaten in favor of worshipping the sun disc, interpreted by the Pharaoh as a god and dubbed with the name of Aten. Having associations with the sun may have been in the Sphinx's favor during this time, as not only was the great monument left unmolested but Pharaoh Akhenaten and his wife Nefertiti were themselves depicted as sphinxes in the decorations of a villa dating to the Amarna Period. Further repairs and renovations on both the Great Sphinx of Giza and its associated temples were carried out by later rulers Seti I and Ramesses II. Ramesses II even added base reliefs to the Sphinx temple depicting himself making offerings to the Great Sphinx.

---

[61] Markowitz, Yvonne; Haynes, Joyce & Freed, Rita. 2002. *Egypt in the Age of the Pyramids.* Museum of Fine Arts, Boston Expedition, Boston, USA.

A ceremonial beard was also added to the face of the Sphinx, although it is uncertain when, since the addition of the beard ended up falling away later on.[62]

Aten shines light on a sphinx of Akhenaten

By the 26th Dynasty, the masonry of the Sphinx was noticeably crumbling away, and a major repair program saw limestone blocks encasing the structure once more. Even the Romans couldn't resist assisting the monument's preservation, adding a series of stones the size of contemporary bricks to the body of the Sphinx where severe erosion had set in. Use of soft white colored limestone for these repairs has meant that the repair material has fared worse over the passage of time than the original monument itself, but they can still be seen in some sections of the Sphinx to this day.

The story of the Sphinx through the ages is, therefore, one of repair and care from the many rulers of Egypt that followed its initial construction. Alas, not all time periods have been so kind, as in modern eras vandalism has joined the forces of erosion in the ongoing decay of this great monument. One of the most obvious, and thus most talked about, elements of vandalism on the Great Sphinx of Giza is the loss of its nose. Tour guides in Egypt often talk of Napoleon in this regard, regaling travelers with stories of his army firing their canons at the Sphinx and succeeding in dislodging its nose with one of their more accurate shots. While it is true that the armed forces of Napoleon's expedition did use the monument for some sessions of target practice, as did later armies such as Mameluk troops and the British Army, it is more generally accepted that the nose was lost due to the intentional efforts of a Muslim zealot sometime around 1378 A.D. The zealot was one Muhammad Sa'im al-Dahr, a Sufi Muslim who was living in Cairo at the time. The story goes that he flew into a rage after witnessing peasants from Egypt presenting the Sphinx with offerings, asking the "talisman of the Nile" for its assistance in delivering a bountiful harvest. Full of righteous anger, he apparently vandalized the monument

---

[62] Hill, J. 2010. *The Great Sphinx of Giza*. Site accessed 14 July 2013. http://ancientegyptonline.co.uk/great-sphinx.html

by destroying the Sphinx's nose, irrevocably changing the appearance of the ancient statue forever.[63]

Al-Dahr was allegedly hanged for his vandalism, but further vandalisms were to follow in later years as well, as the search for treasure led many to deface the monument in various ways. The treasure hunting sea captain Giovanni Caviglia, for example, cleared all the sand from around the Sphinx's chest in 1818, thus uncovering the long buried stele of Thutmose IV. This uncovering of the monument gave access to another treasure hunter in 1838, surveyor and engineer John Shae Perring, who was convinced that there was treasure hidden within the Sphinx itself and searched repeatedly for a way in. This included drilling holes into the body of the Sphinx. Although the holes themselves caused what appeared to be only limited destruction, their legacy was unfortunately more long term and widespread across the monument. The holes allowed for water to seep into the statue's body during rain, which contributed to its ongoing destruction until the holes were eventually fixed in the 1920s.[64] Preservation would later come to be a major factor in the way the Sphinx was approached and understood, but such heritage concerns came much later, after science, Egyptology and archaeology came to define the way people saw the vast monuments of Egypt's past.

[63] Hill, J. 2010. *The Great Sphinx of Giza*. Site accessed 14 July 2013. http://ancientegyptonline.co.uk/great-sphinx.html
[64] Papanek, John (editor). 1992. *Egypt: Land of the Pharaohs*. Time Life Books, USA. pp 66.

A portrait of Perring

Chapter 4: Napoleon and the Science of Egyptology

The development of Egyptology and the science of archaeology emerged out of a popular fascination with the relics of the past, part of a craze of romanticism that has at various times been applied to varying parts of the world and its mysterious past. Fascination with Egypt's antiquity took the form of treasure hunting before scientific curiosity and a respect for the artifacts of past cultures came to the forefront.

In the case of Egypt, these strands of interest have been traced back to one event: Napoleon's military expedition to Egypt in 1798. The French general was leading a campaign against Turkish forces then present in Egypt, bringing with him 34,000 troops to do so. Ironically, given his reputation for damaging the Sphinx, Napoleon also brought a team of 167 artists and scientists, and it was these men who led the effort to systematically record the remnant features of ancient Egypt. The troops were even utilized to clear sand away from around the base of the Sphinx, although less scientifically it is also reported that they used the ancient edifice for target practice prior to undertaking military maneuvers. Napoleon attempted to inspire his troops by referring to the ruins of the past surrounding them prior to their march into battle. He reportedly said, "Soldiers! From the summit of yonder pyramids forty centuries look down upon you."

Jean-Léon Gérôme's famous painting, *Bonaparte Before the Sphinx* (1867-8)

Thanks to Admiral Horatio Nelson and British forces, Napoleon's military expedition was not a success for Napoleon, but the scientific outcome was nothing less than extraordinary, with a 24 volume text titled Description de l'Egypte being the result.[65] The scholarly collection of information was the first of its kind, and upon returning to Europe it was this that produced the interest of so many. Scholars, artists, antiquarians and scientists from across Europe and America began to descend upon Egypt as a result. Some came to solve its mysteries, while others came to

---

[65] Papanek, John (editor). 1992. *Egypt: Land of the Pharaohs.* Time Life Books, USA. pp 34.

plunder its past, but for all and sundry the Sphinx was there, watching and waiting as the world's attention became increasingly focused on Egypt.

Drawings of the Sphinx from Description de l'Egypte

Unfortunately, the earliest arrivals were often more concerned with treasure than knowledge. Characters like Giovanni Battista Belzoni were common, an Italian strongman who liaised with tomb robbers in order to gain access to the valuables of the past buried throughout Egypt. The majority of his experiences destroyed more than they illuminated, with him casually describing crushing sarcophagi in his stumbling rush through tombs, or even cooking roast chicken for dinner on a fire heated by fragments of broken sarcophagi, bones and other mummified remains.[66] Such misadventures were commonplace in a time period where excavation was more likely to be conducted by dynamite rather than brush and trowel. As a monument rather than a temple or tomb, the Great Sphinx of Giza remained relatively unscathed, but the occasional rumor that it housed a secret cache of treasure worked to its disadvantage, as per the drilling of holes in its body in 1838 by surveyor and engineer treasure-hunter John Shae Perring. It took time for scientific knowledge to presage treasure as the main motivation for study in Egypt, and even now tales of the treasure hunter era flavor contemporary understandings of archaeology and Egyptology.

A portrait of Giovanni Battista Belzoni

Archaeology, to take the term on its most commonly accepted level, is a discipline concerned with the past that achieves its outcomes through examination of artifacts associated with human manufacture or which carry evidence of human contact and interaction. While it is true that most

---

[66] Belzoni, Giovanni Battista. 1820. *Narrative of the operations and recent discoveries within the pyramids, temples, tombs, and excavations, in Egypt and Nubia; and of a journey to the coast of the Red Sea, in search of the ancient Berenice, and of another to the oasis of Jupiter Ammon.* J. Murray, London.

archaeologists agree on these basic premises, the gradations of difference surrounding the key concepts are paramount. Archaeology is many things to many people and has a plethora of specialized subsets within it. Some examples include: Rescue Archaeology, Experimental Archaeology, Historical Archaeology, Industrial Archaeology, Prehistoric Archaeology, Processual Archaeology, Post-processual Archaeology, Theoretical Archaeology, Landscape Archaeology, Feminist Archaeology, Fringe Archaeology, Popular Archaeology, Consultant Archaeology and Biblical Archaeology, to name but a few key examples from a much longer list. Agendas, theories, methods and motivations will differ between the many archaeologists that take part in works crossing into these subset areas. An Industrial archaeologist looks at different time periods than a Prehistoric archaeologist, and a Post-Processual archaeologist has a different set of values, ideals and intentions than a Processual archaeologist. Even within these so-called groups individuals will disagree with each other regarding the nature, intention, best working method and theoretical approach to be taken as an archaeologist. One archaeological theorist named Johnson stated that these groups are "actually a very diverse set of concerns and ideas that coalesced around certain slogans" and the blanket overarching term is not a referent for uniformity, but rather "conceals a great diversity of viewpoints and traditions".[67]

Further differences can be noted with different cultural backgrounds, as with French, German and Dutch teams, for example, each having their own cultural approaches towards excavation techniques and documentation, being the result of training undertaken from a particular cultural background. It is often the case in sciences that key concepts are agreed upon but most everything else is fair game for debate and discussion. For some, archaeology is a kind of storytelling,[68] for others it is detective work,[69] to some an art,[70] to some a science[71] and to some merely a science of rubbish.[72] While there are those who have claimed in the past that archaeology is a subset of other disciplines, such as history[73] or anthropology,[74] such claims carry little weight in contemporary times and owe more to the origins of the discipline than to what it has since become. Archaeology is no more a handmaiden to history[75] than it is a treasure hunting adventure,[76] although the echoes of these early avenues and instances still color the discipline as it continues to develop. Archaeologist Chang stated that "as a tool archaeology serves many masters"[77] and it is important to remember that while one archaeologist may focus

[67] Johnson, Matthew. 1999. *Archaeological Theory – An Introduction*. Blackwell Publishers, UK. pp 101.
[68] Nelson, Sarah Milledge (ed). 2006. Archaeological Perspectives on Gender. In: Nelson, Sarah Milledge (ed). 2006. *Handbook of Gender in Archaeology*. AltaMira Press. USA. pp 9.
[69] White, Peter. 1974. *The Past is Human*. Angus and Robertson. Great Britain.
[70] Braidwood, Robert J. 1970. Quoted in: Cleator, P. E. 1976. *Archaeology in the Making*. St Martin's Press, New York.
[71] Ely, Talfourd. 1890. Quoted in: Cleator, P. E. 1976. *Archaeology in the Making*. St Martin's Press, New York.; Biek, Leo. 1963. Quoted in: Cleator, P. E. 1976. *Archaeology in the Making*. St Martin's Press, New York.
[72] Fagan, Brian M. 1978. *Archaeology – A Brief introduction*. Little, Brown and Co. Boston, Toronto. pp 2.
[73] Courbin, Paul. 1972. Quoted in: Cleator, P. E. 1976. *Archaeology in the Making*. St Martin's Press, New York.
[74] Crawford, O. G. S. 1953. Quoted in: Cleator, P. E. 1976. *Archaeology in the Making*. St Martin's Press, New York.
[75] Daniel, Glyn. 1950. *A hundred and fifty years of Archaeology*. Redwood Burn Ltd, Throwbridge and Esher. Great Britain. pp 9.
[76] Papanek, John (editor). 1992. *Egypt: Land of the Pharaohs*. Time Life Books, USA. pp 18-19.

on reconstructing human actions of the past,[78] another may be more interested in large scale, long term material change traced through monuments, structures and settlement patterns.[79] Archaeology allows for multiple approaches, and considering the differing finds, conditions, challenges and contexts encountered on archaeology sites around the world different approaches, theories and intentions are very appropriate.

As the archaeologist Knudson stated, "archaeology is a complex, scientific discipline which encompasses many levels of inquiry and many varied goals".[80] As to the more philosophical questions of what archaeology is and does, each archaeologist will have their own point of view. Joukowsky is more personal when discussing the need for archaeology, stating: "the essence of archaeology is that it makes our world much more meaningful… Archaeology deepens our understanding of humanity and society… it uplifts us by satisfying our basic desire and need to know who we are".[81] This deals with the philosophy of why there is a need for archaeology and gives insight into Joukowsky's own personal motivations and inspirations as an archaeologist. Fletcher and Bailey, on the other hand, look at the specific strengths of archaeology when defining their approaches, examining what archaeology can do that no other discipline can. Artifacts of great variety abound throughout the many environments of earth, some as large as 100 square kilometres, some as small as a fraction of a millimetre, some millions of years old, others as recent as yesterday. Fletcher and Bailey both point out that they form a consistent record of long-term human interaction with material, something that archaeology is uniquely positioned to effectively examine.[82] How that record is then used to reason about the past is a matter for ongoing debate and conjecture.

Although it is generally accepted in archaeology and Egyptology that Khafre was the pharaoh responsible for the construction of the Great Sphinx of Giza, there is still some ongoing debate about the matter. The evidence for Khafre consists of the proximity of his own pyramid to the monument, as well as the facial similarities of the Sphinx to other representations of Khafre from Egypt's archaeological record. The so-called dream stele of Thutmose IV has also been cited as referring to Khafre, but damage to the inscription means that this is also open to debate. It was

[77] Chang, K. C. 1978. Some theoretical issues in the archaeological study of historical reality. In: Dunnell, Robert C. and Hall Jnr, Edwin S. (eds). 1978. *Archaeological essays in honour of Irving B. Rouse.* Mouton Publishers. The Hague, The Netherlands. pp 13.

[78] Movius, Hallam L. 1965. Quoted in: Cleator, P. E. 1976. *Archaeology in the Making.* St Martin's Press, New York.

[79] Bailey, G.N. 1983. Concepts of time in Quaternary prehistory. In: *Annual Review of Anthropology.* Volume 12: 165-192. Annual Reviews, USA. pp 165; Fletcher, Roland. 1986. Settlement Archaeology: world-wide comparisons. In: *World Archaeology.* Number 18 (1): 59-83.; Fletcher, Roland. 1995. *The Limits of Settlement Growth.* Cambridge University Press.

[80] Knudson, S. J. 1978. *Culture in Restrospect: An Introduction to Archaeology.* Rand and McNally College Publishing Company. Chicago. pp 4-5.

[81] Joukowsky, Martha. 1980. *Field Archaeology.* Prentice Hall Inc, New Jersey. pp 1.

[82] Fletcher, Roland. 1995. *The Limits of Settlement Growth.* Cambridge University Press. pp 188; Bailey, G.N. 1983. Concepts of time in Quaternary prehistory. In: *Annual Review of Anthropology.* Volume 12: 165-192. Annual Reviews, USA. pp 165.

archaeologist Thomas Young who noted Khaf written in hieroglyphs within a damaged cartouche, the design of which is usually utilized to denote a royal name, but by the time the stele was re-examined in 1925, the Khaf reference had been destroyed due to further flaking. Counter evidence to the Khafre hypothesis include another inscription, called the Inventory Stela, describing Khufu discovering the Sphinx already buried in sand during his era. This would mean that the Sphinx is even centuries older than previously thought, but the Inventory Stela dates to somewhere between 678 and 525 B.C., so the inscription has been interpreted as a revisionist story from the Late Period, making it an example of the propaganda of the past, with the ancient Egyptians rewriting their own already ancient history . Writer Colin Reader weighed the evidence and concluded "the execution of the Inventory Stela is poor and the names used for the various deities mentioned in the text are clearly those employed during the Late Period... [it is] a fraudulent attempt on the part of the Late Period Egyptians to re-discover a past which was, even then, of great antiquity."[83]

Archaeologist Rainer Stadelmann, who was once the director of the German Archaeological Institute in Cairo, stated the case against Khafre as the builder of the Sphinx through examination of the monument's iconography and surrounding architecture. Khafre's Causeway, he argued, was built around a pre-existing structure, with Stadelmann arguing based on location that the pre-existing structure was the Great Sphinx of Giza itself. Therefore, he reasoned, if the monument predated Khafre, its iconography would be indicative of an earlier period. Stadelmann argued this different iconography included the headdress or nemes of the Sphinx, as well as the one-time beard that has long since been detached from the monument along with its nose. The iconography of both beard and headdress, Stadelmann argued, were stylistically similar to the era of Pharaoh Khufu, reigning between 2589 and 2566 BCE.[84] As the builder of the Great Pyramid of Giza and father to Khafre, Khufu is a popular choice for alternate interpretations of the pharaoh who oversaw the creation of the Sphinx.

With that said, Stadelmann's argument of the causeway being built around an existing structure does not take into account the fact that the outcrop the Sphinx was carved from would have been a natural feature present in the landscape long before it was shaped into the likeness of the Sphinx. In other words, the causeway could have been constructed even before the Sphinx was finished, thereby making it possible that Khafre was responsible for both the Sphinx and the causeway. Despite the dissenting views, current consensus among Egyptologists is that Khafre was the pharaoh who instigated the sculpting of the Sphinx monument from a natural outcrop, left over following the completion of his father's Great Pyramid of Giza. Although this position may change if further evidence is acquired, it remains the most commonly accepted version of the past at this time.

[83] Reader, Colin. 2002. *Giza Before the Fourth Dynasty*. Journal of the Ancient Chronology Forum #9. pp 5–21. Site accessed 14 July 2013. http://www.thehallofmaat.com/modules.php?name=Articles&file=article&sid=93

[84] Stadelmann, Rainer. 2003. The Great Sphinx of Giza. In: Hawass, Zahi (editor). *Egyptology at the Dawn of the Twenty-First Century: Proceedings of the Eighth International Congress of Egyptologists*. American University in Cairo Press, Cairo and New York. pp. 464-469.

Chapter 5: The Sphinx and Pop Culture

In addition to the literature of archaeology, there is another arena where the Sphinx continues to loom large, inspiring a vast array of different stories, images and ideas. That arena is, of course, popular culture, where the story of the Sphinx continues to both assert and reshape itself, much as it once did in Greek mythology so long ago. Public fascination with Egypt and the mysteries of its past have led to the development of a variety of novels, films, games and comics which explore the mythological and fictional aspects of that history. As a primary figure within the landscape of the past, the Sphinx has become a focal point for much of these explorations. Much as Greek mythology took the image of the Sphinx to represent the old world in the tale of Oedipus, so contemporary fiction wraps notions of magic, evil curses and forgotten knowledge around that same image, juxtaposing the modern world against the otherness of Egypt's fictional past.

One example of this is the short story "Under the Pyramids", published in the pulp magazine *Weird Tales* in February 1924. The story outline came from none other than Harry Houdini, who pitched an allegedly true tale of his own encounter with strange forces in Egypt to magazine editor J. C. Henneberger. Attracted to the idea of attaching Houdini's name to his magazine, Henneberger readily agreed and quickly commissioned a regular contributor to ghost write the story. That writer was none other than the iconic fantasy and horror author H. P. Lovecraft, whose own Cthulu tales of elder gods threatening to wake from an other-dimensional slumber and return to this Earth have been disturbing readers worldwide for decades. Lovecraft chose to write the short story in the first person, presenting it as though Houdini himself were telling the tale. Indeed, some published versions of the story did not include a credit for Lovecraft, choosing instead to present the fiction as a true event in the life of the great escape artist, written by him alone.

The story is set in 1910 and tells of Houdini encountering a tour guide with a striking resemblance to one of the ancient pharaohs of Egypt. The guide kidnaps Houdini and takes him to the Great Sphinx of Giza, where the escape artist is thrown into a deep hole located nearby the famous monument. Luckily Houdini is made of stern stuff and is able to escape from this predicament through the industrious use of his techniques in escapology. However, as he is making his way through darkened passages, searching for the way out, he comes upon a vast cavern, decorated as a place of ancient ceremony and possibly as one of sacrifice, with Houdini himself having been the next intended victim. For there, deep beneath the ground, is a vast and terrible creature, the real beast that the Sphinx monument was based upon, still alive and hungry in the dark beneath the hot sands of the Egyptian desert.[85] Lovecraft's telling of the tale places it in the context of his Cthulu stories, giving it a dark and mythic resonance which Houdini apparently enjoyed, collaborating with Lovecraft on further projects thereafter. The mysteries of

---

[85] Lovecraft, H. P. & Houdini, Harry. 1924. *Under the Pyramids. Weird Tales May –July 1924.* Weird Tales, USA.

ancient Egypt, such a source of fascination to the general public, are answered here in fiction as the Sphinx is given a living counterpart, a disturbing deity of immense power, somehow darker and more disturbing than the one that Oedipus so famously defeated through his intellect. Other writers have also written the Sphinx as a living creature, but not always with the sense of horror and darkness that Lovecraft preferred.

One writer who wrote about the Sphinx with humor was British author Terry Pratchett, who created his own version of ancient Egypt within a fantasy setting known as Discworld. The Discworld was a flat land in the shape of a disc, supported on the backs of giant elephants who themselves were standing on the shell of a vast turtle that was swimming through space. The inhabitants of the Discworld were a motley assortment of wizards, witches and barbarians in a comedy mash-up of classic fantasy tales. Within that invented world was also Pratchett's own version of Egypt, where he was able to parody various aspects both of Egyptian history and, more to the point, popular culture interpretations of it.

In the Pratchett book *Pyramids*, the story's hero, pharaoh and sometime assassin Teppic, faces off against the Sphinx in a separate plane of reality. As in the mythological story of Oedipus the Sphinx delivers its challenge, asking the famous riddle: "What has four legs in the morning, two legs in the middle of the day, and three legs in the evening?" Faced with the prospect of being eaten if he answers incorrectly, yet not knowing the answer, Teppic instead questions the logic of the riddle itself. "Is there internal consistency within the metaphor?" he asks of the Sphinx, questioning if all of the stated elements really did happen to one individual in the space of one day. Once the sphinx admits the allegorical nature of the challenge, Teppic presses on, pointing out logical problems. If a human lifespan, roughly estimated to average to about 70 years, is compressed to the period of a single day, then the amount of time spent as a baby crawling on all fours would only be twenty minutes rather than the entirety of the morning. Besides which, that period in a 24 hour day is actually just after midnight and can hardly be referred to as morning anyway. Besides, not all elderly people require walking sticks, while some might need more than one in order to help them get around.

Teppic subsequently offers to help the Sphinx rewrite the riddle in order to increase the allegorical accuracy of it. For example, he suggests, instead of the "three legs in the evening" bit, it would surely be better to phrase it as: "after supper-time it continues to walk on two legs or with any prosthetic aids of its choice". Of course, by the time the logic of riddle has been exposed, Teppic has learned the answer and is able to provide it and go on past the monstrous Sphinx unscathed.[86]

The use of the riddle from Greek mythology in the context of a fictional story soaked in Egyptian imagery demonstrates how much a part of the character of the Sphinx that mythological reference has now become. From the perspective of the present, the various accumulations of

[86] Pratchett, Terry. 1989. *Pyramids*. Corgi, Doubleday, Great Britain; Pratchett, Terry & Simpson, Jacqueline. 2008. *The Folklore of Discworld*. Corgi, Doubleday, Great Britain.

history have attached themselves to the image of the Sphinx, shaping its mythology in ways that make contemporary understandings of it into something that would have been completely alien to the people that built the monument so many years ago.

Another series that plays with the established facts of history is Asterix, a French comic book series set in the year 50 B.C., just as the entirety of Gaul has been conquered by Julius Caesar. All of it, that is, except for one small village, where the local druid brews a magic potion that endows the drinker with superhuman strength. The main characters, Asterix, his best friend Obelix and pet dog Dogmatix, travel throughout the conquered Roman empire meeting various historical figures and creating mayhem along the way. Their visit to Egypt, for example, in the story 'Asterix and Cleopatra', was a good excuse to explain just what happened to the Sphinx's nose, with Obelix accidentally knocking it off while climbing up the Sphinx to get a better view of the area.[87] This is typical of the fun the series has with history, which is certainly successful at getting younger readers interested in learning more about the past; any historical knowledge based on Asterix in isolation however is bound to be misguided at best. This form of playfulness with the mysteries of the Sphinx is not uncommon in fiction, with various versions presented of how it lost its nose and whose face the monument was based upon. In the British science fiction series *Doctor Who*, for example, the time travelling Doctor discovers that his companion Peri has convinced the ancient Egyptians to use an image of Elvis as their basis for the Sphinx in the story "The Eye of the Scorpion".[88]

Other aspects of ancient Egypt continue to flavor the Hollywood approach to retelling the past in films such as *The Mummy*, a 1932 horror movie[89] with a family friendly franchise remake version from 1999.[90] Both films and the multitude of others like them utilize notions of ancient curses and reanimated corpses wrapped in peeling linen bandages to intrigue a modern audience already fascinated with the unknown mysteries of the ancient past. As a symbol the Great Sphinx of Giza epitomises this fascination and is a recurring icon of it. Fictional representations of the modern world have continued what the ancient Greeks began with their own mythological reinterpretation of the creature represented by the ancient monument. It is not inconceivable to guess that this process of reinterpretation and reinvention will continue long into the future, but while the verbal meaning continues to shift, filtered through the vision of changing audiences over time, the monument that inspired all the stories stands constant, worn by time but otherwise unyielding as the many interpretations of it wash like water across its heavy stone features.

---

[87] Goscinny & Uderzo. 1969. Asterix and Cleopatra. Brockhampton Press Ltd, Great Britain.
[88] McLaughlin, Iain. 2001. *Doctor Who – The Eye of the Scorpion*. Big Finish, UK.
[89] Freund, Karl (director). 1932. *The Mummy*. Universal Pictures, USA.
[90] Somers, Stephen (director). 1999. *The Mummy*. Universal Pictures, USA.

Chapter 6: Tourism

The Sphinx in 2010

The Great Sphinx of Giza is a powerful image of the ancient world, an enduring symbol of contemporary Egypt, and one of the cornerstones drawing a range of modern travelers from across the globe to indulge in the tourist experience. Of course, it is not just the Sphinx that tourists like to visit, since they can take in the surrounding temples as well as the pyramids that dominate the Cairo skyline, but the Sphinx itself is a central icon and part of the panorama of spectacle that attracts so many. They come by bus and cab, usually making the trip out from nearby Cairo to Giza. Some may even choose to walk the distance if they are fit enough and wanting to add a pilgrimage feel to their travels. Other visitors travel with organized tours, making their way amongst the lines of open-mouthed and wide-eyed viewers snaking through the monuments and back again, shepherded by protective guides who help them find their way, avoid souvenir sellers and converse in the local language.

The tradition of tourism in Egypt has a long history, and the ancient world had its fair share of travelers as well, many of whom marveled at the icons of a past that was already ancient even to them. This tradition first started around the 4th century B.C. after the Greek culture spread across what was then the known world. Civilizations previously controlled by the Persians, Babylonians and Egyptians became more readily accessible to Hellenistic travellers, leading to the compilation of a definitive lists of sights that had captivated those who had gone there before them. There were multiple lists of must-see items compiled by such travelers as the historian Herodotus, the epigrammist Antipater of Sidon, and the architect Callimachus of Cyrene, and the lists of structures and landmarks were utilized as guidebooks for those tourists who followed.

Over time, the varying documents formed one compilation comprising what mathematician Philo of Byzantium called The Seven Sights of the World, better known now as the Seven Wonders of the Ancient World. These wonders comprised the Hanging Gardens of Babylon, the Temple of Artemis at Ephesus, the Statue of Zeus at Olympia, the Colossus of Rhodes, the Mausoleum at Halicarnassus, the Lighthouse of Alexandria and the Great Pyramid of Giza.[91] Of all these ancient wonders, only one remains intact, the Great Pyramid of Giza, still standing today and continuing to draw further tourists even after all these centuries.

The Great Sphinx of Giza is not on the list of seven wonders, and the absence of such a prominent feature has sparked questions for many. The Greek historian Herodotus records many details about the pyramids and temples of Egypt but makes no mention of the Sphinx at all in his voluminous works.[92] This has led some to hypothesize that the Sphinx may well have been buried in drifts of sand during the 5th century B.C., which would mean that it would not have featured in the collective memory of those ancient tour groups.[93] However, later commentators from antiquity were aware of its presence. One was the Roman Gaius Plinius Secundus, more popularly known as Pliny the Elder, who lived from 23-79 A.D. A writer, philosopher, military commander, naturalist and traveler, Pliny the Elder wrote down his own observations of the Great Sphinx of Giza during a visit to Egypt and referred to the monument as representing a divinity. He also made reference to the structure as a tomb, citing it as being the final resting place of King Harmais, who Pliny described as being buried within it. Although Pliny the Elder's knowledge in this regard was erroneous and was no doubt composed of stories formed from the fragmented memories of the populace, his observations at least suggest that the Sphinx made a dramatic emergence from the sands sometime after the 5th century B.C.[94]

In contemporary times, many tour companies and hotels have styled themselves after the vast statue, both by name and design. It is far from uncommon to book a trip with Sphinx Travel or Sphinx Tours, or to stay at Mercure Cairo le Sphinx, the Sofitel Le Sphinx, Sphinx Guest House or the Sphinx Resort Hotel. The iconography associated with the Sphinx has firmly affixed itself to the marketing of Egypt and is a central feature of the tourist images, journals and blogs that result from the voluminous number of visitors each year. More than 12.8 million tourists went to Egypt in 2008, providing nearly $11 billion U.S. dollars in revenue, and in the year 2010 it was estimated that over 14 million tourists visited Cairo. However, the numbers dropped to nine million in 2011 due to uprisings across the region and remained low after that due to ongoing political uncertainty. Nevertheless, despite these issues, the flow of tourism has never stopped.

[91] Clayton, Peter & Price, Martin. 1988. *The Seven Wonders of the Ancient World.* Routledge, USA. pp 162–163.

[92] Herodotus (translated by Grene, David).1988. *Herodotus – The History.* University Of Chicago Press, USA.

[93] Wilson, Andrew. 2013. *Oedipus & the Sphinx - The Riddle of the Sphinx. The Classics Pages.* Site accessed 28 June 2013. http://www.users.globalnet.co.uk/~loxias/sphinx.htm

[94] Pliny (translated by John Bostock and Henry Thomas Riley). 1857. *The Natural History of Pliny.* H. G. Bohn, London. pp 336–337.

Its importance to the economy of Egypt is without question, with estimates on tourist receipts calculated as fluctuating between $2,942,000,000 in 1998 up to $13,633,000,000 in 2010. It has been estimated that the tourist sector employs approximately 12% of the overall Egyptian workforce.[95]

However, the importance of tourism for economic benefit has to be balanced against the damage that associated urban growth and development does to the monuments of the past that the people want so desperately to see. In 2008, for example, there was enough concern about the rising water table beneath the Sphinx to establish an in-depth study of the situation. Three months of comprehensive ecological and geophysical studies by the Archaeological Engineering Centre of Cairo and Ain Shams universities determined that inadequate drainage systems in the suburb of Nazlet Al-Semman were causing the water table to rise and salt to accumulate on the surface of the ground facing the Sphinx's Valley Temple. The encroaching suburbs getting closer and closer to the Sphinx and pyramids were a direct result of growing tourist numbers causing a need for growth and expansion.[96] Some of the developments that led to the rising water included the public gardens and residential area of Hadaaq Al-Ahram, along with the golf course at the Mena House Hotel. The solution was the installation of a pumping system to reduce the high rate of subterranean water accumulation through 18 water pump machines across the plateau. It was estimated in 2012 that these machines were pumping out 26,000 cubic metres of water per day at a rate of 1,100 cubic metres of water every hour.[97]

The importance of the Great Sphinx of Giza ensures it will be protected and preserved for as long as possible, and it has already stood the test of time far longer than many other monuments and artifacts of the ancient world. As Lehner put it, "The Sphinx is the oldest patient in the world." Indeed, it has pervaded history, legend and popular culture, and what once was modern has since become ancient beneath its gaze. Perhaps even the modern world will one day look ancient to the Great Sphinx of Giza, one of a handful of constants within an ever changing landscape. But what is certain is that tourists will continue traveling to see it and people will continue to debate its history and origins.

Bibliography

Al-Ahram. 2008. *Dammed, but not drowning.* Site accessed 28 June 2013. http://weekly.ahram.org.eg/2008/891/he3.htm

Al-Ahram. 2012. *Rising water: a necessary evil?* Site accessed 28 June 2013.

---

[95] Index Mundi. 2013. *Egypt - International tourism, number of arrivals.* Site accessed 28 June 2013.
    http://www.indexmundi.com/facts/egypt/international-tourism
[96] Al-Ahram. 2008. *Dammed, but not drowning.* Site accessed 28 June 2013.
    http://weekly.ahram.org.eg/2008/891/he3.htm
[97] Al-Ahram. 2012. *Rising water: a necessary evil?* Site accessed 28 June 2013.
    http://weekly.ahram.org.eg/2012/1105/eg8.htm

http://weekly.ahram.org.eg/2012/1105/eg8.htm

Athenaeus. 1930. *The Deipnosophistae of Athenaeus*. Loeb Classical Library edition, Harvard University Press, USA.

Bailey, G.N. 1983. Concepts of time in Quaternary prehistory. In: *Annual Review of Anthropology*. Volume 12: 165-192. Annual Reviews, USA.

Bauer, S. Wise. 2007. *The History of the Ancient World*. W. W. Norton & Company Inc, New York.

Belzoni, Giovanni Battista. 1820. *Narrative of the operations and recent discoveries within the pyramids, temples, tombs, and excavations, in Egypt and Nubia; and of a journey to the coast of the Red Sea, in search of the ancient Berenice, and of another to the oasis of Jupiter Ammon*. J. Murray, London.

Biek, Leo. 1963. Quoted in: Cleator, P. E. 1976. *Archaeology in the Making*. St Martin's Press, New York.

Bodsworth, Jon. 2011. *Egypt Archive*. http://www.egyptarchive.co.uk

Braidwood, Robert J. 1970. Quoted in: Cleator, P. E. 1976. *Archaeology in the Making*. St Martin's Press, New York.

Chang, K. C. 1978. Some theoretical issues in the archaeological study of historical reality. In: Dunnell, Robert C. and Hall Jnr, Edwin S. (eds). 1978. *Archaeological essays in honour of Irving B. Rouse*. Mouton Publishers. The Hague, The Netherlands.

Clayton, Peter & Price, Martin. 1988. *The Seven Wonders of the Ancient World*. Routledge, USA.

Courbin, Paul. 1972. Quoted in: Cleator, P. E. 1976. *Archaeology in the Making*. St Martin's Press, New York.

Crawford, O. G. S. 1953. Quoted in: Cleator, P. E. 1976. *Archaeology in the Making*. St Martin's Press, New York.

Daniel, Glyn. 1950. *A hundred and fifty years of Archaeology*. Redwood Burn Ltd, Throwbridge and Esher. Great Britain.

Dodson, Aidan & Hilton, Dyan. 2004. *The Complete Royal Families of Ancient Egypt*. Thames & Hudson.

Ely, Talfourd. 1890. Quoted in: Cleator, P. E. 1976. *Archaeology in the Making*. St Martin's

Press, New York.

Encyclopædia Britannica. 2013. *Khafre*. Site accessed 14 July 2013.
http://www.britannica.com/EBchecked/topic/316035/Khafre

Fagan, Brian M. 1978. *Archaeology – A Brief introduction*. Little, Brown and Co. Boston,
Toronto.

Fletcher, Roland. 1986. Settlement Archaeology: world-wide comparisons. In: *World
Archaeology*. Number 18 (1).

Fletcher, Roland. 1995. *The Limits of Settlement Growth*. Cambridge University Press.

Freund, Karl (director). 1932. *The Mummy*. Universal Pictures, USA.

Goscinny & Uderzo. 1969. *Asterix and Cleopatra*. Brockhampton Press Ltd, Great Britain.

Hadingham, Evan. 2010. Riddle of the Sphinx. Cosmos Magazine. Site accessed 8 July 2013.
http://www.cosmosmagazine.com/features/riddle-sphinx/

Herodotus (translated by Grene, David). 1988. *Herodotus – The History*. University Of
Chicago Press, USA.

Hill, J. 2010. *The Great Sphinx of Giza*. Site accessed 14 July 2013.
http://ancientegyptonline.co.uk/great-sphinx.html

Index Mundi. 2013. *Egypt - International tourism, number of arrivals*. Site accessed 28 June
2013. http://www.indexmundi.com/facts/egypt/international-tourism

Johnson, Matthew. 1999. *Archaeological Theory – An Introduction*. Blackwell Publishers, UK.

Joukowsky, Martha. 1980. *Field Archaeology*. Prentice Hall Inc, New Jersey.

Knudson, S. J. 1978. *Culture in Retrospect: An Introduction to Archaeology*. Rand and
McNally College Publishing Company. Chicago.

Lehner, Mark. 1985. *The Pyramid Tomb of Hetep-heres and the Satellite Pyramid of Khufu*.
Mainz am Rhein, Germany.

Lovecraft, H. P. & Houdini, Harry. 1924. *Under the Pyramids. Weird Tales May –July 1924*.
Weird Tales, USA.

Markowitz, Yvonne; Haynes, Joyce & Freed, Rita. 2002. *Egypt in the Age of the Pyramids*.
Museum of Fine Arts, Boston Expedition, Boston, USA.

McLaughlin, Iain. 2001. *Doctor Who – The Eye of the Scorpion*. Big Finish, UK.

Movius, Hallam L. 1965. Quoted in: Cleator, P. E. 1976. *Archaeology in the Making*. St Martin's Press, New York.

Nelson, Sarah Milledge (ed). 2006. Archaeological Perspectives on Gender. In: Nelson, Sarah Milledge (ed). 2006. *Handbook of Gender in Archaeology*. AltaMira Press. USA.

Papanek, John (editor). 1992. *Egypt: Land of the Pharaohs*. Time Life Books, USA.

Pliny (translated by John Bostock and Henry Thomas Riley). 1857. *The Natural History of Pliny*. H. G. Bohn, London.

Pratchett, Terry. 1989. *Pyramids*. Corgi, Doubleday, Great Britain.

Pratchett, Terry & Simpson, Jacqueline. 2008. *The Folklore of Discworld*. Corgi, Doubleday, Great Britain.

Reader, Colin. 2002. *Giza Before the Fourth Dynasty*. Journal of the Ancient Chronology Forum #9. pp 5–21. Site accessed 14 July 2013. http://www.thehallofmaat.com/modules.php?name=Articles&file=article&sid=93

Science Dump. 2012. *The Riddle of the Sphinx*. Site accessed 28 June 2013. http://www.sciencedump.com/content/riddle-sphinx

Somers, Stephen (director). 1999. *The Mummy*. Universal Pictures, USA.

Sophocles. 1991. *Oedipus Rex*. Dover Thrift Editions, Dover Publications, USA.

Stadelmann, Rainer. 2003. The Great Sphinx of Giza. In: Hawass, Zahi (editor). *Egyptology at the Dawn of the Twenty-First Century: Proceedings of the Eighth International Congress of Egyptologists*. American University in Cairo Press, Cairo and New York.

Time Life Books. 1987. *The Age of God-Kings*. Time Life Books Inc, USA.

White, Peter. 1974. *The Past is Human*. Angus and Robertson. Great Britain.

Wilson, Andrew. 2013. *Oedipus & the Sphinx - The Riddle of the Sphinx*. The Classics Pages. Site accessed 28 June 2013. http://www.users.globalnet.co.uk/~loxias/sphinx.htm

Zivie-Coche, Christiane. 2002. *Sphinx: History of a Monument*. Cornell University Press.

The Hanging Gardens of Babylon

Chapter 1: A Wonder of the Ancient World

The Hanging Gardens of Babylon were such a sight to behold that they featured prominently even among the very earliest lists of the seven wonders of the ancient world. The idea of listing the seven wonders of the world is one that developed in ancient Greece and remains popular in the imagination of the Western world today. The natural world is full of majesty and wonder that causes people to look on in astonishment and awe, but the ancient Greeks reserved their highest praise for monumental human achievements, works that, like the fabled Tower of Babel, would cause the gods to fear that humanity has learned to work together in such harmony that nothing will be impossible for them.

Although the Hanging Gardens and the company they kept are universally known today as the Seven Wonders of the Ancient World, the group of seven were not originally labeled as "wonders" (*thaumata* in Greek), but as "sights" (*theamata* in Greek) (Clayton and Price, 1988, 4). They were included in ancient Greek travel guides as the must-see destinations for affluent travelers who were curious to see the best of what the rest of the world had to offer. This conceptualization of such "sights" was typified by Herodotus, the 5th century B.C. Greek historian. In his life's work, the *Histories*, Herodotus speaks fondly of the city of Babylon and of Egypt and its pyramids, though it must be noted he did not make any specific mention of hanging gardens.

The Greeks had a high regard for tradition, antiquity and wealth, and it was abundantly clear that the Egyptian and Babylonian civilizations possessed each of these qualities. When Alexander the Great conquered the Persian armies and wrested control of their great empire for himself in the 4th century, there was a major emphasis on what united the eastern and western parts of his empire. It was during this Hellenistic period that the fascinating sights (*theamata*) became "wonders" (*thaumata*). It was no coincidence that the locations of the original seven wonders not only fell within the confines of Alexander's empire but also marked the vast expanse of it.

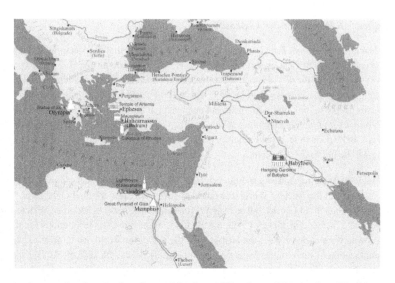

A map showing the locations of the Seven Wonders of the Ancient World

Callimachus of Cyrene wrote a work in the 3rd century B.C. entitled "A Collection of Wonders in Lands throughout the World." All that remains of this work is the name of it, but the title itself indicates Greek writers were compiling lists of remarkable human achievements. The most recently built "wonder" that made the canonical list of seven was the statue of Helios in Rhodes, which was completed during Callimachus's lifetime, though it is impossible to say whether such a recent work of craftsmanship made it into Callimachus' work.

Whatever the case, by the mid-2nd century B.C., the list of seven had become fixed. These seven were preserved in a poem written by Antipater of Sidon, which reads:

> "I have gazed on the walls of impregnable Babylon,
>
> along which chariots may race,
>
> and on the Zeus by the banks of the Alpheus,
>
> I have seen the Hanging Gardens
>
> and the Colossus of Helios,
>
> the great man-made mountains of the lofty pyramids,
>
> and the gigantic tomb of Maussollos.

But when I saw the sacred house of Artemis that towers to the clouds,

the others were placed in the shade,

for the sun himself has never looked upon its equal outside

Olympus." (Antipater, *Greek Anthology*, IX 58)

While the poet sets apart the temple of Artemis from the rest of the list, in many ways the Hanging Gardens stand out as a mystery within this list. There are no outstanding questions about the other wonders in terms of what they are, when they were constructed, or where they are located, yet the Hanging Gardens present anomalies in each of these areas. Ancient visitors who presumably would have or should have seen such a marvelous sight remain silent on the matter, and modern archeologists excavating the site fumble around in trying to identify any trace of such an agricultural feat among the city's remains. Assyriologists continue to search in vain for any firsthand or primary references to this wonder that clearly astounded generations of Greeks. But historians love these kinds of mysteries, which allow them to don their detective hats and try to come up with an explanation.

Chapter 2: Ancient Descriptions of the Hanging Gardens

Despite a lack of primary sources, there is certainly no lack of secondary sources, as the Hanging Gardens appear in a half a dozen or so ancient Greek sources. Moreover, while the descriptions differ in some minor details, they largely agree on the main points.

It is important to keep in mind that although they shared a great deal in common in terms of their writing system and their religion, the Assyrians and the Babylonians were two distinct cultural groups with distinctive empires in ancient Mesopotamia. They can be thought of as very similar to the Greek and Roman empires in terms of cultural proximity. They spoke different but closely related languages, they had similar pantheons (with different names for the same deities), and the geographic extent of their empires overlapped a great deal at their peaks. Various native Babylonians in the 4th and 3rd centuries B.C. set to writing histories of the Assyrian and Babylonian empires for consumption by Greek audiences, who appreciated ancient civilizations and religious rituals. Thus, most of the surviving sources referring to the Hanging Gardens came secondhand from Greek authors quoting works by these native authors.

It is worth reviewing the actual Greek sources that speak of the Hanging Gardens in chronological order, but even here, there's a problem in deciding upon the chronological order of these sources. For example, they could be aligned by the dates of the sources themselves, or they can be aligned by the dates of the primary sources referred to. This chapter is arranged by looking at the chronological order of the sources referred to by the Greek writers.

From 60-30 B.C., an ancient Greek historian named Diodorus Siculus wrote historical works, and he relied on a history of Alexander the Great written by Cleitarchus of Alexandria in the 4th century B.C. Relying on that source, Diodorus Siculus wrote about the Hanging Gardens:

> "There was also, beside the acropolis, the Hanging Garden, as it is called, which was built, not by Semiramis, but by a later Syrian king to please one of his concubines; for she, they say, being a Persian by race and longing for the meadows of her mountains, asked the king to imitate, through the artifice of a planted garden, the distinctive landscape of Persia. The park extended four plethra on each side, and since the approach to the garden sloped like a hillside and the several parts of the structure rose from one another tier on tier, the appearance of the whole resembled that of a theatre. When the ascending terraces had been built, there had been constructed beneath them galleries which carried the entire weight of the planted garden and rose little by little one above the other along the approach; and the uppermost gallery, which was fifty cubits high, bore the highest surface of the park, which was made level with the circuit wall of the battlements of the city. Furthermore, the walls, which had been constructed at great expense, were twenty-two feet thick, while the passageway between each two walls was ten feet wide. The roofs of the galleries were covered over with beams of stone sixteen foot long, inclusive of the overlap, and four feet wide. The roof above these beams had first a layer of reeds laid in great quantities of bitumen, over these two courses of baked brick bonded by cement, and as a third layer a covering of lead, to the end that the moisture from the soil might not penetrate beneath. On all this again the earth had been piled to a depth sufficient for the roots of the largest trees; and the ground, when leveled off, was thickly planted with trees of every kind that, by their great size or any other charm, could give pleasure to the beholder. And since the galleries, each projecting beyond another, all received the light, they contained many royal lodges of every description; and there was one gallery which contained openings leading from the topmost surface and machines for supplying the gardens with water, the machines raising the water in great abundance from the river, although no one outside could see it being done." (*Library*, 2.10)

Some interesting facts to note from this earliest source are that the queen for whom the garden was built is not named, aside from the specification that it was not Semiramis. This suggests that a lot of people in Diodorus' day were claiming Semiramis as the queen in question.

Furthermore, the reference to the Syrian king is actually an English translation issue. The Greek word syros was confusingly translated by scholars from an earlier generation as "Syrian". In fact, the word syros was a reference to Assyrian; Herodotus clarified the situation when he wrote, "The Greeks call these people Syrians, but others know them as Assyrians."

The emphasis in the description is in the mountain-like quality of the gardens. There is also reference to a water-raising device for irrigation, but no details appear on the specifics of such a device. The first known engineering device that could raise water from a source was the Archimedes Screw, named after the famous 3rd century genius from Syracuse. Archimedes, widely hailed as antiquity's greatest scientist, lived about 400 years after the Hanging Gardens were supposedly built.

Another description that is believed to have come from the 4th century B.C. was related by Strabo, who wrote his famous work *Geography* around 20 B.C. Historians believe that Strabo relied on a history of Alexander the Great written by Onesicritus in the 4th century. Strabo relays the following comments:

> "Babylon, too, lies in a plain;...The garden is quadrangular, and each side is four plethra in length. It consists of arched vaults, which are situated one after another, on checkered cube-like foundations. The checkered foundations, which are hollowed out, are covered so deep with earth that they admit of the largest of trees, having been constructed of baked brick and asphalt—the foundations themselves and the vaults and the arches. The ascent of the uppermost terrace-roofs is made by a stairway; and alongside these stairs there were screws, through which the water was continually conducted up into the garden from the Euphrates by those appointed for this purpose, for the river, a stadium in width, flows through the middle of the city; and the garden is on the bank of the river." (*Geography*, XVI 1.5)

Like the previous description, this description also gives the impression of a mountain-like terrace. It also contains similar descriptions of the foundations of the garden and mentions the water-raising device. This time, Strabo specifically uses the term "screw" to describe the device. Both sources reference the river as the source of the water for the gardens.

The next source in this chronological order is Quintus Curtius Rufus, who wrote a history of Alexander the Great himself. He is also believed to have drawn on Cleitarchus of Alexandria, like Diodorus before him, as well as another 4th century writer named Ctesias. Rufus has the following comments to make about the Hanging Gardens,

> "On the summit of the citadel are the Hanging Gardens, a trite theme with the Greek poets; they equal in height the walls of the town, and their numerous lofty trees afford a grateful shade. The trees are twelve feet in circumference, and fifty feet in height: nor, in their native soil, could they be more productive. Supporting these are twenty dense walls, distant from each other twenty feet, surmounted with ranges of stone piers, over which is extended a quadrangle pavement of stone, strong enough to bear earth amassed high, and water supplied for irrigation. A distant spectator of these groves would suppose them to be woods nodding on

their mountains. Notwithstanding time destroys, by insensible corrosion, not only human works, but even nature herself; yet this pile, pressed with the roots, and loaded with the trunks of so gigantic a plantation, still remains entire. Tradition affirms, that a king of Assyria, reigning in Babylon, executed this work to gratify his queen, who, delighting in forest scenery, persuaded her husband to imitate the beauties of nature by a garden on this imperial scale." (*History of Alexander*, V 1.35)

In this account, there is once again an emphasis on the mountain-like nature of these gardens, and the first description's seemingly confusing reference to a Syrian king is here clarified as an Assyrian who ruled the city of Babylon.

The next source is the Jewish historian Josephus, who wrote in the 1st century A.D. He quotes Berossus, a native Babylonian source dating from the 3rd century BCE. It is this Berossus who provides Josephus with the information on the Hanging Gardens that Josephus incorporated into two of his works. In the context of describing the Babylonian king Nebuchadnezzar II and his accomplishments, Josephus wrote:

"At his palace he had knolls made of stone which he shaped like mountains and planted with all kinds of trees. Furthermore, he had a so-called pensile paradise planted because his wife, who came from Media, longed for such, which was custom in her homeland. (*Jewish Antiquities* X, 11)

...and, within this palace he erected lofty stone terraces, in which he closely reproduced mountain scenery, completing the resemblance by planting them with all manner of trees and constructing the so-called Hanging Garden; because his wife, having been brought up in Media, had a passion for mountain surroundings." (*Contra Apionem* I, 19)

An engraving on an eye stone of onyx with an inscription of Nebuchadnezzar II.

Here, for the first time, the unnamed queen and king are actually identified, and this progression is noteworthy, because it is typical of the growth of legends and should immediately make readers cautious about the reliability of this new information. Josephus also highlighted the mountain-like nature of these gardens.

The latest surviving ancient Greek source to mention the Hanging Gardens is Philo of Byzantium, the Paradoxographer. He lived in the 4th century A.D. and wrote a Greek treatise on the Seven Wonders of the World (Dalley and Oleson, 2003, 11 n. 29). Included in this treatise is a lengthy description of the Hanging Gardens. The most recent translation of this text is quoted below:

> "The so-called Hanging Gardens have plants above ground, and are cultivated in the air, with the roots of the trees above the (normal) tilled earth, forming a roof. Four stone columns are set beneath so that the entire space through the carved pillars is beneath the (artificial) ground. Palm trees lie in place on top of the pillars, alongside each other as (cross-)beams, leaving little space in between. This timber does not rot, unlike others; when it is soaked and put under pressure it swells up and nourishes the growth from roots, since it incorporates into its own interstices what is planted with it from outside. Much deep soil is piled on, and then broad-leaved and especially garden trees of many varieties are planted, and all kinds of flowering plants, everything, in short, that is most joyous and pleasurable to the onlooker. The place is cultivated as if it were (normal) tilled earth, and the growth of new shoots has to be pruned almost as much as on normal land. This (artificial) arable land is above the heads of those who stroll along through the pillars. When the uppermost surface is walked on, the earth on the roofing stays firm and undisturbed just like a (normal) place with deep soil. Aqueducts contain water running from higher places; partly they allow the flow to run straight downhill, and partly they force it up, running backwards, by means of a screw; through mechanical pressure they force it round and round the spiral of the machines. Being discharged into close-packed, large cisterns, altogether they irrigate the whole garden, inebriating the roots of the plants to their depths, and maintaining the wet arable land, so that it is just like an ever-green meadow, and the leaves of the trees, on the tender new growth, feed upon dew and have a wind-swept appearance. For the roots, suffering no thirst, sprout anew, benefitting from the moisture of the water that runs past, flowing at random, interweaving along the lower ground to the collecting point, and reliably protects the growing of trees that have become established. Exuberant and fit for a king is the ingenuity, and most of all, forced, because the cultivator's hard work is hanging over the heads of the spectators." (translation by Dalley, 2013, 40-41)

There are several new elements in this latest description. Like all of the Greek writers mentioned so far, Philo is not believed to have visited Babylon firsthand but likely collected his material from other literary sources. Most striking in this description is the sharp change in description of the gardens, from mountain-like to a description of plants directly above spectators' heads. This aspect of the description, which seems to be implied by the name "Hanging Gardens", is noticeably absent from each of the earlier descriptions, leading to questions over the actual name "Hanging Gardens" itself.

Chapter 3: The Translation of the Name "Hanging Gardens"

The term "Hanging Gardens" has been ubiquitous for nearly 2,000 years, but one of the problems that English speakers have in conceptualizing the Hanging Gardens comes from the name itself. The English word "hanging" evokes for most readers images either of a floating garden with suspended plants or at least ivy-type plants that themselves 'hang' below the roots that secure them. In *The Hanging Gardens of Nineveh*, Karen Foster lists three different possibilities for how these gardens might have been "hanging":

> "(1) trees and bushes grow on substantial structures, looming or hanging above the head of the viewer; (2) vines trail over the edges of rooftops, terraces, and pergolas, again looming or hanging above the head of the viewer; and (3) plants grow in a sunken area, such that the viewer looms or hangs over the garden, even as the plants appear to be suspended or hanging without visible means of support." (Foster, 2004, 209)

The Greek word, *kremastos*, is an adjective derived from the root verb *kremaō*. The verb and adjective are used to describe people "hanging" from the gallows and objects "hanging" from peoples' necks. But interestingly, the Septuagint translation of the Book of Ezekiel provides the closest parallel to this context. The prophet Ezekiel is painting a word picture in his oracle about the king of Judah being taken to Babylon, and the English translation of the Greek Septuagint at this point reads as follows:

> "Therefore, this is what the Lord says:
>
> And it is I who will take some
>
> from the select parts of the cedar;
>
> I will snip off something
>
> from the top of their heart.
>
> And it is I who will transplant

on a high mountain.

And I will hang (*kremasō*) him

in a mountain of Israel high in the air.

And I will transplant him,

and he shall produce a shoot and bear fruit

and become a large cedar." (Ezek. 17:22-23, Pietersma, 2007, 959)

In the Hebrew original, the verb at the end of verse 22, translated by the Greek translators as "transplant", is the same exact verb that they translated as "hang" at the beginning of verse 23. The Hebrew verb, *šātal*, is one of several Hebrew verbs meaning "to plant", but its meaning is very specific. It is not a native word in Hebrew but was borrowed from Akkadian during the Babylonian captivity. The verb only appears in the works of Jeremiah, Ezekiel and two late psalms. The noun, *šitlu*, refers to offshoots of vines and trees. The verb that was formed from this noun essentially means "to make an offshoot". In other words, it suggests planting or transplanting an offshoot of a tree or vine in a cultivated setting where it would not grow otherwise. When this passage is viewed in light of the adjective for the famous gardens at Babylon, a hitherto unrecognized technical meaning becomes evident. In addition to their standard verb for "transplant," the Greek translators used a technical term for planting a tree on a hilly terrace.

It is in light of the Ezekiel passage that the Greek phrase "hanging gardens" makes more sense, and there is no need to turn to the three possible interpretations of the usual sense of "hanging" outlined by Foster in order to understand the construction and nature of these gardens. The Greek phrase "hanging gardens" likely referred to artificially planted gardens that were set on a slope.

This coincides with all of the classical sources that survived antiquity. The relevant passages read as follows. According to Strabo, "It consists of arched vaults which are located on checkered cube-like foundations. The ascent of the uppermost terrace-roofs is made by a stairway..." Philo makes similar comments, "The hanging garden has plants cultivated above ground level, and the roots of the trees are embedded in an upper terrace rather than in the earth. The whole mass is supported on stone columns..." The longest passage in this regard comes from Diodorus Siculus: "...and since the approach to the garden sloped like a hillside and the several parts of the structure rose from one another tier on tier, the appearance of the whole resembled that of a theatre. When the ascending terraces had been built, there had been constructed beneath them galleries which carried the entire weight of the planted garden and rose little by little one above the other along the approach; and the uppermost gallery, which was fifty cubits high, bore the highest surface of the park, which was made level with the circuit wall of the battlements of the city."

In each case, the author emphasizes the sloping and hill-like nature of the artificial and man-made structures in which the plants and trees grew. It is this feature that the "hanging" likely described, and as such, the description of Philo of Byzantium is most likely an error. Given this context, Philo's description reads more like an unwarranted elaboration by a writer who had not visited the garden itself. Unfamiliar with the technical term and its use in agricultural contexts, Philo of Byzantium used the broader meaning of the Greek term to let his imagination run wild.

Chapter 4: The Legend of Semiramis and the Hanging Gardens

Before diving into the anomalies and inconsistencies regarding the Hanging Gardens, it is important to first establish what the legend was regarding the origins of the Hanging Gardens.

In Classical Antiquity, there were actually two competing legends explaining these origins. In the early 4th century B.C., a Greek physician and historian named Ctesias wrote a 23-book history of Assyria and Babylon after being employed at the royal Persian court. The work is so rife with extraordinary legends and unbelievable tales that historians generally dismiss most of what Ctesias had to say out of hand, unless there is some compelling reason to accept what he says based on corroboration from other sources. Unfortunately, this latter situation rarely arises.

Ctesias describes a great Assyrian queen named Semiramis who is a veiled personification of the Assyrian goddess Ishtar. Like Ishtar, she was a warlike princess who attracted many lovers, almost all of whom she treated with contempt and cruelty. According to Ctesias, Semiramis was married to a king named Ninus (the founder of Nineveh), and she becomes the source of most of the Babylonian architectural structures that remained until Ctesias' time. (Gilmore, 1887, 98) According to the legend, it is she who founds Babylonia and builds roads, bridges and canals throughout the region. She also conquers Egypt, Ethiopia and Media, and she is the one responsible for the Akkadian portion of the Behistun inscription of Darius I carved on the famous wall relief (Schmitt, 1993, 444).

The Behistun inscription

It is in this context that Semiramis is also credited with the construction of the Hanging Gardens. This material, credited to Ctesias, was only preserved in the writings of the 1st century B.C. writer Diodorus Siculus.

The second competing tradition was passed down by Josephus, the Jewish historian living in the Roman Empire during the 1st century A.D. He wrote a great deal about the Jewish scriptures in an attempt to make them accessible to the Roman mind, and a significant amount of material in the Hebrew Bible revolves around the Jewish exile and captivity in Babylon. As such, Josephus wrote about Babylon frequently.

Josephus had been trained in the Roman tradition of collecting multiple oral and written sources for his historical accounts, so he learned about and made use of a native Babylonian history that a Babylonian priest named Berossus had written four centuries earlier. That said, it is doubtful that he had direct access to this work; it seems more likely that Josephus relied on other historians who themselves had read Berossus' work and cited it.

Regardless, Josephus credits Berossus with the information that he relates about Nebuchadnezzar II (Nabouchodonosorous) and the Hangings Gardens. Nebuchadnezzar is said to have constructed stone terraces planted with multiple varieties of trees and the Hanging

Garden in an effort to reproduce the mountain scenery that his Median wife, Amytis, daughter of King Umakishtar, missed so dearly. The Medes were an ancient civilization of Iranian descent, and though native Babylonian sources make no mention of the names of the wives of Nebuchadnezzar II, it is known that he married a Median princess before he was even crowned king.

Another Greek author and contemporary of Josephus, Quintus Curtius Rufus, made similar remarks in his *History of Alexander*, but there is a curious difference in wording. According to Quintus Curtius Rufus, it was "an Assyrian king, reigning in Babylon" who built the Hanging Gardens. At first blush, this would also seem to line up perfectly with Nebuchadnezzar II. It was Nebuchadnezzar's father, Nabopolassar, who succeeded in making Babylon an independent state once again after overthrowing the Assyrian domination that had been a daily part of life in Babylon since it was sacked and raided by Sennacherib several generations prior. Nabopolassar was able to accomplish his goal because he was himself an Assyrian official posted in Babylon at the time. Thus, since Nebuchadnezzar II was Nabopolassar's son, he could have been described as an Assyrian ruling in Babylon.

Unfortunately, there are gaping holes in the historical and literary record that cast doubt upon both legends.

Chapter 5: Discrepancies, Anomalies and Contradictions

If Nebuchadnezzar II had the Hanging Gardens built at Babylon for his wife, as the legend goes, then these gardens should have constituted a prominent feature of the landscape of the city. Just as visitors and travelers commented on the other wonders when they visited those cities, one would expect effusive praise and detailed descriptions of these gardens whenever the topic of Babylon came up. After all, the authors who did mention the gardens described at length and in great detail both the beauty of the sight and its technical ingenuity.

However, multiple reliable authors exclude this expected feature from their descriptions of Babylon, its landscape, and environs. Herodotus described Babylon in great detail, and he mentions the walls of Babylon, its palaces, its temples, and the customs associated with these temples, but he didn't make a single mention of these famed gardens. The absence is so glaring that Stephanie Dalley, a scholar at Oxford University who has pioneered the recent research into the Hanging Gardens, entitled one of her recent articles, "Why Did Herodotus not Mention the Hanging Gardens of Babylon?" In this article, Dalley begins by affirming a fact that late 19th century scholars doubted, that Herodotus likely did visit Babylon and have firsthand knowledge of the city. She goes on to demonstrate that the Neo-Babylonian empire to which Nebuchadnezzar II belonged considered itself the continuation of the Neo-Assyrian empire by pointing to various attempts to maintain a sense of continuity between the two dynasties. After making these two important points, Dalley asks her original question again, "Why did Herodotus not mention the Hanging Gardens?"

Other well-known ancient historians are also silent on the matter. No mention of the Hanging Gardens appears in the *Cyropaedia* by Xenophon either. This work was a biography of sorts of Cyrus the Great, and Babylon figures prominently as one of the empires that Cyrus destroyed. Here again, the absence of any mention of the Hanging Gardens is glaring.

In addition to those two famous Greek writers, several renowned Roman historians fail to mention the existence of the gardens. In Plutarch's biography of Alexander the Great, there is nothing about the Hanging Gardens. Perhaps just as surprising is the description of Babylon in Pliny the Elder's *Natural History*, where he describes the walls of Babylon and the great temple of Jupiter Bel but makes no mention of the Hanging Gardens. The Hanging Gardens, as described in other classical sources, are exactly the type of topographic feature that Pliny set out to describe for readers, yet they do not even warrant a nod from him.

After taking the time to summarize all of the available classical descriptions of the Hanging Gardens, the scholar E. A. Wallis Budge found them to be so self-contradictory that he declared emphatically, "In my opinion a Garden of this size and kind never existed at Babylon" (Budge, 1920, 298). However, historians are quite used to their ancient sources being at odds with each other on various details; after all, if history were so straightforward, even fewer historians would be able to make a living sorting these questions out.

E. A. Wallis Budge

A consideration of the historical topography of the region creates another formidable problem in relation to the Hanging Gardens. One of the reasons why archaeologists have had a field day in Mesopotamia is that the land is so flat that the rivers do not remain in a fixed course for long.

They were continually diverted into new courses in antiquity by either natural phenomena, such as flooding in the wet season, or artificially engineered changes in direction. For this reason, ancient cities that were originally built along the course of the river became abandoned and desolate centuries later if the river had changed its course.

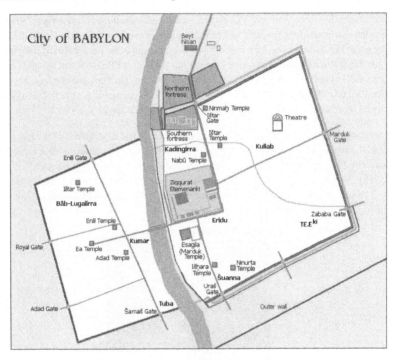

The layout of the city of Babylon in Nebuchadnezzar's time, with the palace complex in the middle.

In the case of Babylon, it was built along the Euphrates River and relied heavily upon the river for transportation of goods, which were sent on barges down the river, as well as its general water supply. The ancient descriptions of the Hanging Gardens indicate that its irrigation system was dependent upon the river, which obviously makes sense, but there are several historical problems based on the following facts. About a quarter of a century after the death of Nebuchadnezzar II, the Persians, led by Cyrus the Great, captured the city of Babylon in 539 B.C. As part of their military campaign to force Babylon to submit, the Persians diverted the Euphrates River away from the city, and it remained in its diverted course for centuries afterward, so that it no longer flowed through the palace complex (Dalley, 1994, 46). If the Persians diverted the river away from Babylon in the 6th century, how could 4th century sources like Ctesias and Berossus describe to their Greek audience a Babylonian garden watered by a river that was no longer there?

In the late 19th century, before archaeologists had excavated the vast caches of cuneiform tablets that can now be found in the British Museum, the Louvre and other famous museums throughout the world, the classical sources were the closest one came to the ancient Babylonian world. But now, a century and a half later, tens of thousands of these Babylonian cuneiform tablets have been deciphered and translated by scholars. Naturally, those translating the tablets figured that there would be a mention of such gardens by the Babylonians themselves, seeing as how they should have been a point of pride that would've inevitably peppered historical inscriptions and letters. Yet the Babylonian records remain silent on the matter of the Hanging Gardens. One text in particular, entitled the Topography of Babylon, would be the ideal place for the Babylonians to rave about their impressive Hanging Gardens, because this text takes up five cuneiform tablets and describes streets and temples and palaces of Babylon in great detail, yet the tablet says nothing about these famous gardens. Not only are the texts silent on the Hanging Gardens in particular; gardens and the act of gardening in general was not a subject that took any pride of place in the Babylonian texts available to us. Whereas the silence on the part of the classical sources is curious but not necessarily damning, the silence from native sources should give everyone pause.

The silence here is not only limited to the literary sources but extends to the archaeological record as well. Mesopotamia is one of the most professionally excavated regions in the world, and the city of Babylon, including the main palace complex, has been excavated extensively. Naturally, the first excavation team, led by Robert Koldewey, attempted to both identify and reconstruct the location of the Hanging Gardens within the palace complex. But ultimately, his identification and reconstruction were so faulty that just about every subsequent archaeologist and historian has torn it apart. The original excavation was unable to make a solid identification of the location of the Hanging Gardens, and no subsequent proposal for the location of the Hanging Gardens in Babylon has been able to garner any significant support.

Koldewey

All of this has ensured that the Hanging Gardens of Babylon are the most mysterious of all of the traditional Seven Wonders of the Ancient World. Given the unlikelihood that multiple ancient sources invented something out of thin air with alarmingly matching details, there was probably some magnificent garden in Mesopotamia connected with a queen that astonished the Greeks and the Romans. Yet the classical sources contain significant unexpected gaps in what they relate about the Hanging Gardens within other descriptions of the city of Babylon, and the topography of Babylon changed so significantly in terms of its water supply after the time of Nebuchadnezzar II that it could not have continued to support any such garden within the palace complex either. The Babylonian literature itself lacks any clear or even obscure or indirect reference to the Hanging Gardens, and the archaeology of the city of Babylon shows no trace of such a structural complex.

This led researchers to one inevitable question: where would the Hanging Gardens of Babylon have been located if not in Babylon?

Chapter 6: Does Babylon Actually Mean Babylon?

The gaps in the historical record, and the lack of evidence in the archaeological record, presented quite a conundrum for those looking for signs of the Hanging Gardens of Babylon, but eventually, work done in the late 20th century tried to make some sense out of the incomplete puzzle.

On the face of it, asking whether the "Babylon" in the Hanging Gardens of Babylon actually referred to the famous city itself is absurd. After all, Babylon was a well-known city in Mesopotamia and served as the capital of the Babylonian empire for most of its existence. On the other hand, the confusion evident both in the ancient sources and the modern archaeological record concerning the Hanging Gardens indicates that an innovative solution along these lines might just be warranted.

Eventually, Assyriologist Stephanie Dalley asked this bold question that previous scholars had not bothered to ask because it seemed nonsensical. She looked at the classical sources with an eye to whether they confused the city of Babylon or possibly conflated it with any other city, and she didn't have to look long before she found plenty of evidence to this effect. The first important source that she discovered in this connection was a series of astronomical observations from Azarqiel of Toledo written in Aramaic. This document makes reference to the longest day of the year from the perspective of "Old Babylon." In and of itself, this would not have been a very significant reference, except when it is combined with the identification of the latitude from which the observation must have been made. Based on the latitude calculations, the "Old Babylon" to which this document referred is not the ancient city of Babylon everyone thinks of today but actually the Assyrian city of Nineveh.

If there are ancient references to "Old Babylon," it begs the question as to the intended referent of its counterpart "New Babylon." Dalley painstakingly outlined how and when these names came into use within the native Akkadian sources themselves. When Assyrian leader Sennacherib sacked and destroyed Babylon in 689 B.C., his army smashed or removed all of the cult statues of the prominent gods within the city. This left the city godless, with no king and in a state of ruin for a quarter century or so, while its former inhabitants lived in exile. It was Sennacherib's son, Esarhaddon, who set to work rebuilding Babylon in an attempt to restore it to its former glory. The restored city that rose out of the ashes of the old was then appropriately dubbed the "New Babylon."

But this leaves the problem of when exactly Nineveh would have been referred to as Babylon. Although other kings adopted the title "king of Babylon" after they defeated the city, Sennacherib did not participate in this naming convention. Instead, for evidence that Nineveh was called Babylon, Dalley turns to the technical history of the textual tradition of one of the most prominent Akkadian myths: Enuma Elish, the Epic of Creation. In the traditional Old Babylonian version of this epic, Marduk defeats Tiamat and establishes Babylon as the center of the universe. In the Assyrian version of this Epic, the god Marduk, who was the traditional god of Babylon, has been replaced by Assur, the eponymous deity of the city of Assur and the Assyrians. What Dalley draws attention to is the fact that although the Assyrians took the time to change the name of the deity who forms the hero of the epic, they left the name of the city that he founded, Babylon, unchanged. For Dalley this makes little sense. If they were concerned about Assyrianizing the epic, why stop at the name of the deity and leave the Babylonian capital as the center of the world?

To answer the question, Dalley theorizes that the Assyrianizing process took place during the period of Sennacherib's reign, and that while the actual Babylon lay in ruins and was godless, the Assyrians began to call Nineveh by the name Babylon. After all, if Nineveh was referred to as Babylon, there would be no need for any further change to the text of the myth, because the renaming of Nineveh to Babylon would make it the center of the world. The god Assur, as the hero of the epic, now establishes Babylon as the center of the world, and Babylon now refers to Nineveh.

Of course, a trained historian is fully aware that a historical argument based on literary evidence such as this could not stand on its own without further support. To provide such support, Dalley garnered more evidence from several economic documents dated to Sennacherib's reign. The most important thing about these economic documents was the manner in which they were dated. Throughout the history of the two empires, the Assyrian and Babylonian, the two kingdoms used different dating systems. In the Babylonian empire, they used regnal years, such as the third year of King Nebuchadnezzar II's reign. In the Assyrian empire, they used what are called year eponyms, as in the year the king did something. In these economic documents, Dalley noted an interesting shift. Sennacherib's financial transactions were dated using the expected Assyrian system in the first half of his reign, but in the latter years of his reign, after he had sacked and destroyed Babylon, his scribes began using the Babylonian system of dating.

Evidence for the renaming of Nineveh as "Babylon" by the Assyrians appears in some of the surrounding cultures as well. The books of Chronicles in the Hebrew Bible present a retelling of the history of Israel and Judah, and at one point, they describe how the Assyrians took Manasseh captive to their capital city. But when the books name the capital city, they do not use the expected name Nineveh but instead use the name Babylon: "Therefore the LORD brought against them the commanders of the army of the king of Assyria, who took Manasseh captive in manacles, bound him with fetters, and brought him to Babylon" (2 Chr. 33:11). Not only was Babylon not the capital of Assyria, this was the very period when Babylon lay in ruins. As such, it is the exact period when Dalley argues that Nineveh was going by the name Babylon.

In addition to this Judean source, there is also a Greek source that provides evidence for the use of the name Babylon to refer to Nineveh. Diodorus Siculus describes many exploits of a legendary queen, whom he calls Semiramis, and she is identified as an Assyrian queen who is responsible for multiple building projects in "Babylon". At that time, however, the Assyrian rulers did not rule over Babylon, and just as importantly, the actual details of the building projects indicate that these projects were located in Assyria, most likely Nineveh, not Babylon. He wrote that Semiramis decorated her building projects with hunting scenes that included a wide variety of wild animals, and that the queen herself appears on one of these portraits riding horseback and impaling a leopard while her husband spears a lion beside her. As will be discussed further in detail below, this type of hunting and artistic imagery was unique to the Assyrians and did not appear in Babylon or as part of Babylonian art.

Diodorus Siculus' description, on its face, makes little sense, and classical scholars have long struggled to understand why Ctesias, Diodorus' native source, would have made such an elementary error. But in this new light, by recognizing that Nineveh for a time bore the name Babylon, and was referred to as "Old Babylon" when Babylon was rebuilt and became "New Babylon", the story makes perfect sense. An Assyrian queen was responsible for numerous building projects in Nineveh ("Old Babylon"), and the Assyrian style hunting scenes scattered throughout these building projects find a home in Nineveh that they would not have found in Babylon.

With all of this said, it must be acknowledged that in all of Dalley's work on this matter, she has failed to come up with any smoking gun that would remove any doubt as to the use of the name Babylon for Nineveh during Sennacherib's reign. But at the same time, the lack of such a smoking gun also might explain why no one came up with this solution to the problem presented by the Hanging Gardens sooner. The solution also has a great deal of explanatory power, since it reconciles the use of the term "Old Babylon" for Nineveh and helps explain several other historical oddities mentioned above.

Ultimately, the idea of Hanging Gardens themselves actually bolsters the argument that Nineveh was known as Babylon during the reign of Sennacherib, because one of the biggest differences between Nineveh and Babylon was the emphasis on gardening.

Chapter 7: A Regional Emphasis on Gardening and Gardens

Although both Nineveh and Babylon are both situated in what people immediately think of as the dry and arid climate of Mesopotamia, Babylon is located closer to the equator and thus experiences less annual rainfall than Nineveh. Climate maps show that Babylon is located in a region that receives only 100-200 mm of rainfall per year, whereas the city of Nineveh receives 600-1000 mm of rainfall annually. Babylon has a more desert-like climate, while Nineveh is more Mediterranean.

These distinct climate differences also expressed themselves in the distinctive cultures of each region. Understandably, both cultures prized water resources and fostered very adept engineers who mastered the art of controlling the flow of the rivers and developed innovative means for irrigating their fields, but in Babylon, the amount of water was so minimal that the focus of irrigation efforts was almost solely on crop production. The situation in Assyrian Nineveh was markedly different. Although water was still a valuable resource and one that needed to be protected and maximized, the Assyrians used water more freely than their Babylonian counterparts. The Assyrians not only raised crops but also grew ornamental gardens and parks whose purpose was more aesthetic than functional.

Assyrian kings also prided themselves on their hunting ability, which was a quite popular form of entertainment and sport in the royal court, and Assyrian kings built *ambassu*, which were large game parks where such sporting events could take place, and some of the most popular Assyrian reliefs that the general public is familiar with are those involving the king killing lions with a spear and similar weapons. This matches what is depicted in Ctesias' description of the wall that flanked the Hanging Gardens: "The height and width of this wall were even greater than those of the middle wall. On it, and on its towers, there were again wild beasts of every kind, cleverly drawn and realistically colored to represent a complete big-game hunt. These animals were more than 6 feet long, and Semiramis was portrayed among them, mounted and hurling a javelin at a leopard. By her side was her husband Ninus, dispatching a lion at close quarters with his spear." (Macqueen, 1964, p. 158). Such a description does not match any of the Babylonian motifs for art, but is a common theme in Assyrian art.

A bas relief from Sennacherib's palace depicts him during his war against Babylon

Furthermore, the Assyrians developed a strong literary tradition wherein the king would describe how he constructed various gardens in building inscriptions similar to those used for canals, palaces and temples. Not only was there such a strong literary tradition for gardens, but the Assyrian scribes used an interesting phrase in their descriptions of these gardens. They use the phrase *tamšil Ḫamāni* ("in the likeness of the Amanus mountains") to describe these gardens. This phrase highlights the fact that these gardens were not built in the style of the Western gardens of the time that favored symmetry with flowers and trees arranged in a central configuration (Oppenheim, 1965, 332); instead, they were constructed in the relatively flat plains of Assyria to model a hilly and wooded terrain with its winding footpaths and streams. The Assyrian monarchs not only conscripted literary descriptions of these gardens but adorned their palaces with bas reliefs depicting this lush terrain. Keeping these facts in mind, the presence of the Hanging Gardens in a place once called "Old Babylon" (Nineveh) would be entirely in keeping with what is known about the history and the values of the region and the culture. Conversely, trying to fit the Hanging Gardens into the traditional city of Babylon seems like trying to fit a square peg into a round hole.

Moreover, this new perspective helps to shed light on a comment found in Josephus's Babylonian source, Berossus, who talks about Nebuchadnezzar II building stone hills plated with all kinds of trees beside his Babylonian palace. This same Berossus provides one of the key Classical Greek descriptions of the Hanging Gardens. If Berossus had "Old Babylon" (Nineveh) in mind when he wrote about the stone hills and the Hanging Gardens, it would bring a great deal more credibility to the description and would easily explain how a non-native reader like Josephus could have mistaken Nineveh for the Babylon that stood at the center of the Babylonian empire.

Chapter 8: Native Descriptions of a Wonder?

In the 7th century B.C., the Assyrian king Sennacherib used the phrase "as a wonder for all people" (*"ana dagālu kiššat nišū"* in Akkadian) to describe his palace and accompanying gardens (VAB 4 138 ix 30). When dealing with two languages as different as Greek and Akkadian, it's important not to get too hung up on the fact that the same English word is used to translate both phrases from these two languages. What is more important in this context is that the Assyrian king, Sennacherib, thought his palace gardens were awe-inspiring for anyone who saw them, whereas the native Babylonian annals and documents make no such references to gardens and hardly make mention of gardening at all. This isn't that surprising given that the climate of Babylon did not lend itself to parks or gardens. Expending their precious few water resources on such extravagant pursuits as sport and aesthetic enjoyment would have ruined the economy by diverting necessary resources away from the production crops that supplied food for the city.

When Strabo described the Hanging Gardens and its irrigation system in great detail, he used the Greek term *kochlias* ("screw") to describe the mechanism that watered the gardens. This has proved to be another one of the many mysteries associated with the Hanging Gardens. Archimedes, who is generally credited with the invention of the screw as a water-raising device, did not invent this device until around 250 B.C., but it is clear that such a device was being used in Egypt in Ptolemaic times prior to Archimedes' version of the device (Stevenson, 1992, 48). The question is whether that engineering design could have already been in use in Mesopotamia three centuries before Ptolemy ruled Egypt. There was not a great deal of contact between the two civilizations before the 3rd century, and there is little reason to suspect that Greek engineers would have been allowed to study the technology involved in such an irrigation system. Moreover, because the mechanics of the system were internal, mere observation would not be sufficient to grasp and reproduce such technology.

That said, the ancient sources discussing the Hanging Gardens all make mention of some sort of engineering device that could raise water. For instance, Diodorus Siculous wrote, "…and there was one gallery which contained openings leading from the topmost surface and machines for supplying the gardens with water, the machines raising the water in great abundance from the river, although no one outside could see it being done." (Diodorus Siculus, Library 2.10). Unless the ancient accounts relating to the irrigation of the Hanging Gardens are all discounted, it is entirely possible that Mesopotamian agricultural engineers were years ahead of their time. In such an arid climate as Mesopotamia, irrigation technology was a key concern, so it makes sense that a great deal of time and finances were devoted.

Stephanie Dalley has taken this issue one step further. She found Assyrian texts that describe Sennacherib's palace and its associated gardens, and among these texts was a description of new technology for watering these gardens. In this text, Sennacherib uses a word for the hollowed out trunk of a palm tree, *alamittu*, to describe a screw that he used as a water-raising device. He explains how he cast the two separate components of this device using clay moulds, into which he then poured molten copper or bronze (Dalley, 1993, 8). The correspondence between this native Mesopotamian description and the description given by Strabo is striking to say the least. Here there is a Mesopotamian king boasting not only about the opulence and grandeur of his gardens but also the technology used to sustain it.

Scribes described the palace that Sennacherib built for himself as "The Palace without Rival" in multiple inscriptions. Two of these inscriptions were clay prisms, a popular shape of dedicatory inscriptions during the time, and another set were inscribed on a lion-sphinx. The extensive description of the garden associated with this palace appears on the prism inscriptions, and the detailed description of the irrigation system for these gardens appears on the lion-sphinx inscription without the accompanying description of the garden itself.

Perhaps most interesting of all is the dedication that appears on the lion-sphinx inscription immediately following the description of the Archimedean screw-type water-raising device. It reads:

> "And for Tašmētum-šarrat the queen, the chosen bride, my beloved, whose form Belet-ili has made more perfect than that of any other woman, I had a palace of loveliness, joy and happiness made, and so I put female lion-sphinxes of white limestone at its doors. At the command of Assur, father of the gods, and Ištar the queen, may we enjoy a long time together in those palaces in pleasure of the flesh and joy of the heart, may we have our fill of longevity. May a favourable *šedu* and a favourable *lamassu* always encircle the sides of those palaces forever, may their good omens never cease." (Dalley, 2002, 67-68)

Taken in the context of this proposal, Nineveh and Sennacherib would coincide with both traditional legends about the origin of the Hanging Gardens in a broad sense, since the gardens and the palace that they surround at Nineveh were dedicated to a queen. Furthermore, such a dedication of a building and its gardens to a queen is unique within the Assyrian and Babylonian traditions (Dalley, 2002, 68); one has to go to the Hittite or Luwian inscriptions to find anything comparable. This uniqueness only adds to the likelihood of identifying the Hanging Gardens with Sennacherib's garden structures at Nineveh, as opposed to anything built by Nebuchadnezzar II at Babylon.

Chapter 9: Problems with the Nineveh Theory?

Sometimes, in the process of attempting to solve a longstanding historical problem, the innovative solution creates new unforeseen problems once the implications of the new perspective are fully thought through. The situation with the Hanging Gardens is no different. There is no doubt that Dalley's theory that the Hanging Gardens were in Sennacherib's Nineveh, not Nebuchadnezzar II's Babylon, has many compelling points in its favor, but this reassessment of the historical material creates some new problems.

Without question, the most formidable problem relates to the history of Nineveh after Sennacherib, because seemingly all historical sources, including classical, Biblical and Babylonian sources, indicate that the great city of Nineveh met its fate at the hands of a coalition between Nebuchadnezzar II and the Medes in 612 B.C. In fulfillment of Assyrian curses and Biblical prophecies, the city was flooded and entirely destroyed. Thus, this raises a problem similar to the one regarding the diversion of the Euphrates River from Babylon. If Nineveh was ruined in the early 7th century B.C., it is impossible to understand how the magnificent Hanging Gardens were still standing from the 4th century B.C. through the 1st century A.D., when travelers were acclaiming it as one of the Seven Wonders of the World. Quintus Curtius Rufus makes the following comment about the Hanging Gardens as late as the 1st century A.D.: "Notwithstanding time destroys, by insensible erosion, not only human works, but even nature herself, yet this pile, pressed with roots, and loaded with the trunks of so gigantic a plantation, still remains entire."

The literary sources that relate the fall of Nineveh are quite varied in their ideological perspective, but they are in agreement on the major points. Chronologically, the first source is the Biblical prophet Nahum. He predicted the fall of Nineveh in an oracle only a few years before the event took place. The entire book of Nahum contains the superscription, "An oracle concerning Nineveh." Although the entire book of Nahum concerns the downfall of the city, the most relevant passages read as follows:

> "He calls his officers;
>
> They stumble as they come forward;
>
> they hasten to the wall,

and the mantelet is set up.

The river gates are opened,

the palace trembles.

It is decreed that the city will be exiled…" (Nahum 2:5-7)

"Nineveh is like a pool

whose waters run away." (Nahum 2:8)

"The crack of whip and rumble of wheel,

galloping horse and bounding chariot!

Horsemen charging,

flashing sword and glittering spear,

piles of dead,

heaps of corpses,

dead bodies without end—

they stumble over the bodies!..." (Nahum 3:2-3)

"Then all who see you will shrink from you and say,

'Nineveh is devastated; who will bemoan her?'

Where shall I seek comforters for you?" (Nahum 3:7)

"Yet she will become an exile,

she went into captivity;

even her infants were dashed in pieces

at the head of every street;

lots were cast for her nobles,

all her dignitaries were bound in fetters…" (Nahum 3:10)

"...fire has devoured the bars of your gates." (Nahum 3:13, NRSV)

As a forward looking prophecy, this information provides very little reliable information for the historian. Each of these things could have taken place, some of them could have taken place, or none of them could have taken place. The passage about the river gates being opened and Nineveh becoming a pool has been paired with the much later statement from the historian Diodorus Siculus, who states that Nineveh was destroyed in a three-year siege when the Euphrates flooded and breached the walls of the city. The problem with Diodorus' account is that the city of Nineveh does not lie on the Euphrates River but rather on the Tigris. Moreover, the features of the Tigris River would not have allowed it to flood the city as Diodorus described.

Van de Mieroop has studied this account of Diodorus and his source Ctesias and argues that it is not simply that Ctesias was an idiot and did not know what he was talking about. Rather, the Babylonians viewed their successful attack on Nineveh as payback for Sennacherib's attack on Babylon years earlier (van de Mieroop, 2004, 3). As such, the Babylonian literary accounts that described the attack on Nineveh described them as parallel events. In essence, the Babylonians were boasting that they did to Nineveh what Sennacherib had done to Babylon. The flooding of the river was something that happened to Babylon, not necessarily to Nineveh, but to keep the accounts consistent, both cities were said to have been flooded by the river. This style of parallel narratives also helps to explain why Ctesias would have written the wrong name of the river, and also why Ctesias describes a three-year siege of Nineveh, when this was a characteristic of the siege of Babylon, not of Nineveh. While the city was clearly destroyed in 612 B.C., it was not flooded as many historians used to suggest.

The Babylonian Chronicle is probably the most reliable historical account of the destruction of the city, but it is certainly not free of bias. The relevant portion reads as follows:

> "Twelfth year: When, in the month of Abu, the Medians...against Nineveh...they rushed and seized the town of Tarbisu, a town belonging to the province of Nineveh,...they went downstream on the embankment of the Tigris and pitched (camp) against Ashur. They made an attack against the town and [took the town], [the wall of] the town was torn down, a terrible defeat/massacre they inflicted upon the entire population. They took booty (and) carried pri[soners away]...
>
> [Fourteenth year]: The king of Akkad cal[led up] his army and [Cyaxar]es, the king of the Manda-hordes (Umman-manda) marched towards the king of Akkad, [in]...they met each other. The king of Akkad...and [Cyaxar]es...[the...]s he ferried across and they marched (upstream) on the embankment of the Tigris and...[pitched camp] against Nineveh...From the month Simanu till the month Abu, three ba[ttles were fought, then] they made a great attack against the city. In the month Abu, [the ...th day, the city was seized and a great defeat] he inflicted

[upon the] entire [population]. On that day Sinsharishkun, king of Assy[ria fled to]…, many prisoners of the city, beyond counting, they carried away. The city [they turned] into ruin-hills and hea[ps (of debris). The king] and the army of Assyria escaped (however)…" (Pritchard, 1969, 304-5)

Based on the Babylonian Chronicle, it is clear that the city was destroyed and its population decimated, but this begs the question of what happened to the gardens and their structures. Armies do not typically focus on destroying plants and vegetation, so while it is possible that they destroyed anything with an air of beauty about it, that would not necessarily be a foregone conclusion. Many of the measures that they might take to destroy the beauty of the gardens, like chopping down tree limbs or trampling flowerbeds, would be short-lived, and the effects would not last more than a few seasons.

In fact, the archaeological evidence indicates that the city of Nineveh continued to be occupied throughout the last few centuries B.C. and the first centuries A.D. (Stronach and Codella, 1997, 147). A building identified as the Hermes Temple was found in 1954 at the site, and the English translation of the Arabic excavation report reads:

"In October 1954 the custodian of the Nineveh remains directed the attention of Mohammed Ali Mustafa to a piece of limestone he had discovered sticking out of the ground a little more than 100m north of the north-west corner of Nebi Yunis…The area surrounding the shrine was examined. It rose about 1m above the surrounding plain and extended for some distance, in the south running under the newly constructed houses. The high elevation suggests a Hellenistic settlement. This is supported by the discovery three years earlier of a limestone altar of Assyrian origin bearing a cuneiform inscription of Sennacherib on one side and a Greek inscription on the other. The altar was surrounded by pieces of stone and further investigation ascertained that the locality was the site of a large building whose foundations were of large blocks of limestone: perhaps the site of another Hellenistic temple… All these features, pointing towards the existence of a Hellenistic settlement in Nineveh, have been found on the west side of the city…" (Scott and MacGinnis, 1990, 69-70)

The difference in situation between that of the multiple problems for Babylon and the Hanging Gardens as compared with the new problems facing Nineveh and the Hanging Gardens is extraordinary. Whereas digging deeper into the historical evidence regarding Babylon and the Hanging Gardens continued to reveal more and more problems with such an identification, the more historical information researchers learn about Nineveh, the fewer problems exist for locating these famed gardens at Nineveh.

As the various accounts, historical facts, and theories make clear, the Hanging Gardens are by far the most mysterious of the ancient Seven Wonders of the World. Ironically, the ancient sources are fraught with difficulties and contradictions, but the biggest contradictions seemingly vanish when the Hanging Gardens of Babylon actually become the Hanging Gardens of Nineveh. While it might be impossible to ever determine the location of the ancient wonder with certainty, it was at the Assyrian capital that Sennacherib boasted that he constructed a garden to rival all gardens as a wonder for the entire world to see, replete with a description of the innovative water-raising device used centuries before Archimedes made his screw. He even dedicated his palace and the accompanying gardens to his queen and left inscriptions declaring his devotion to her.

If the Hanging Gardens were indeed Sennacherib's feat, it produces one of antiquity's greatest ironies. In Sennacherib's zeal to take all glory from Babylon by sacking the city, hauling off its deities and giving his capital city of Nineveh the name Babylon, he may have inadvertently given credit for one of his proudest accomplishments to his arch-nemesis.

Bibliography

Budge, E. A. Wallis. *By Nile and Tigris: A Narrative of Journeys in Egypt and Mesopotamia on behalf of the British Museum between the Years 1886 and 1913.* London 1920.

Clayton, Peter A. and Martin J. Price. *The Seven Wonders of the Ancient World.* London, 1988.

Dalley, Stephanie. "Ancient Mesopotamian Gardens and the Identification of the Hanging Gardens of Babylon Resolved." *Garden History* 21 (1993) 1-13.

Dalley, Stephanie. "Nineveh, Babylon and the Hanging Gardens: Cuneiform and Classical Sources Reconciled." *Iraq* 56 (1994) 45-58.

Dalley, Stephanie. "More about the Hanging Gardens." Pp. 67-73 in Lamia al-Gailani Werr, et. al. (eds.) *Of Pots and Pans: Papers on Archaeology and History of Mesopotamia and Syria Presented to David Oates in Honour of His 75th Birthday.* London, 2002.

Dalley, Stephanie. "Why Did Herodotus not Mention the Hanging Gardens of Babylon?" Pp. 171-89 in Peter Derow and Robert Parker eds. *Herodotus and His World:*

Essays from a Conference in Memory of George Forrest. New York, 2003.

Dalley, Stephanie. *The Mystery of the Hanging Garden of Babylon: an Elusive Wonder Traced*. Oxford, 2013.

Dalley, Stephanie and John Peter Oleson. "Sennacherib, Archimedes, and the Water Screw: The Context of Invention in the Ancient World." *Technology and Culture* 44 (2003) 1-26.

Foster, Karen. "The Hanging Gardens of Nineveh." (2004)

Gilmore, John. "The Sources of the Assyrian History of Ktesias." *The English Historical Review* 2 (1887) 97-100.

Macqueen, James G. *Babylon*. New York, 1964.

Oppenheim, A. Leo. "On Royal Gardens in Mesopotamia." *Journal of Near Eastern Studies* 24 (1965) 328-33.

Pietersma, Albert and Benjamin G. Wright (eds.). *A New English Translation of the Septuagint*. New York, 2007.

Schmitt, Rüdiger. "Ctesias." Vol. VI/4 pp. 441-46 in *Encyclopædia Iranica*. London, 1993.

Scott, M. Louise and John MacGinnis. "Notes on Nineveh." *Iraq* 52 (1990) 63-73.

Stronach, David and Kim Codella. "Nineveh." Vol. 4 pp. 144-48 in Eric M. Meyers (ed.) *The Oxford Encyclopedia of Archaeology in the Near East*. 5 Vols. New York, 1997.

van de Mieroop, Marc. "A Tale of Two Cities: Nineveh and Babylon." *Iraq* 66 (2004) 1-5.

CPSIA information can be obtained
at www.ICGtesting.com
Printed in the USA
BVOW08s1859261216
471851BV00013B/815/P